Planning for Future Market Events Using Data Processing Support

A FIVE-STEP GROWTH PLAN PROCESS

Jerome Svigals

Macmillan, Inc.
NEW YORK
Collier Macmillan Publishers
LONDON

TO *LIZ*
for encouragement
for patience
for tolerance
WITH LOVE

Macmillan, Inc.
866 Third Avenue, New York, N.Y. 10022

Collier Macmillan Canada, Inc.

Printed in the United States of America

printing number

1 2 3 4 5 6 7 8 9 10

Library of Congress Cataloging in Publication Data

Svigals, Jerome.
   Planning for future market events using data processing support.

   Includes index.
   1. Banks and banking—Data processing.   2. Business—Data processing.   3. Market surveys.   I. Title.
HG1709.S87   1983   332.1′028′54   82-48765
ISBN 0-02-949740-X

Contents

Preface

This book is the result of my 30 years of experience with data processing systems, mostly as an employee of the IBM Corporation. My activities have been in the definition and development of new functional uses for these systems. For the last 16 years I have worked on the development of electronic funds transfer and self-service banking concepts and capabilities.

My successful data processing experiences always seemed to share a set of common characteristics:

○ My experiences depended on a good grasp of a marketplace event or capability to be achieved.

○ The way in which the data processing system served to achieve the market event was set by the needs of the event.

○ The needs of the event and the plan for achievement were documentable.

○ The results of achieving the event were quantifiable and measurable.

○ Preparation started early enough to achieve the event within the time and resources available.

○ The achievement plan allowed managers to set progress milestones and observe the attainment of them.

○ Criteria for movement from one milestone to the next were specified and tested for achievement.

○ The process left room for the unknown and allowed for changes as needed, but within the available resources.

These characteristics of success are almost impossible to find in most situations. They result only from careful planning and preparation. It was from these experiences that the growth plan process evolved.

The growth plan process is intended as an orderly process that provides:

○ Early plans for market events and data processing support

○ A basis for early decisions

○ A process that allows for change

○ A process that easily evolves with progress

My experiences with the growth plan process involved many friends, associates, and business relationships. The knowledge, challenges, and achievements of these IBM and customer groups were the source of very valuable contributions to the development and refinement of this process. It is impossible to single out individual contributions. I feel indebted to them all.

I also want to express my appreciation for the IBM policies and practices for authors. IBM encourages self-development; it encourages the development and application of new concepts; and it encourages the writing of books like this to communicate these concepts. It is a rare privilege to work in such a stimulating environment.

○ CHAPTER ONE
○
○
○ *Introducing*
○
○ *the Growth Plan Process*
○

CHAPTER GOALS

Describe the motivation to understand this subject.

Review the early use and results of this plan process.

Describe the growth plan process.

Discuss the kind of examples to be used.

WHAT IS THE PROBLEM?

A recent article in *Business Week,* entitled "How to buy enough computers," noted that data processing budgets are now growing as large as those of other corporate functions. More important, the functions performed by data processing are rapidly becoming critical to companies. As a result, the data processing manager is now taking an important seat in a growing number of management committees. Furthermore, with data processing systems, there is a fast-moving trend to "interactive" usage.

In interactive applications, users have direct access to electronic processing and electronic access to vital data. These interactive or "on-line" data processing systems handle orders and transactions, maintain inventories and records, and perform other vital business functions. This immediate access quickly makes computers a vital part of doing business. In fact, some companies are essentially betting the success of their business on the capability of their data processing systems. They are betting that the systems will allow them to keep up with the needs of their business.

Availability is a key factor in the ability of these data processing systems to keep up. Availability means that a data processing system is performing the tasks to keep a business running successfully when the system is needed. In short, data processing is becoming a basic and vital fact of corporate life. Adequate capacity and availability must be provided, where and when needed.

If having the right capacity at the right time is vital, then how is it best provided? The best approach is to anticipate and to prepare in advance for future needs. Until now the planning process for data processing systems has usually been haphazard. The management of the data processing system has been considered separate from the marketing and business strategy planning of an organization. To some, this gap between the planning for market needs and for the data processing system is getting wider. Why? Because some key "user" executives remain reluctant to manage their data processing capabilities. To other user executives, reaching out more than 6 months to anticipate market needs is still a magic act. Thus the data processing systems are speeding toward a more central role in the everyday operations of a business, even while the leaders may not be planning the business's future.

Purpose of This Book

The purpose of this book is to close the gap between data processing and business operations. This book describes a future plan process. This growth plan process is designed to help the "using" manager and the data processing manager to jointly understand and control their growing use of data processing systems. This is not a course in data processing. That is left to others. Everything you need to know about data processing for this planning purpose is explained here—or expressed in terms you can understand. Of course understanding data processing concepts is very helpful. But even more helpful is your strong desire to manage and use the data processing function more effectively.

Everyone Is Data Processing Management

The focus of this book is not limited to those who are involved in the functional management of data processing. Effective use of data processing must be the role of all managers and users, at all levels. Thus, a general management point of view is also important to those professionals dealing with data processing from the outside, such as consultants, investors, accountants, financial analysts, bankers, lawyers, and students. They all need to appreciate how the data processing systems may be better integrated into the future plans for a business.

The Growth Plan Process

The growth plan process described in this book offers a proven "cook book" approach. The process is a five-step action plan, as follows:

Step one of the growth plan process is selection of the business areas to be covered. This first step includes setting the time frame or period to be analyzed. Step one also includes selection of the objectives and goals to be satisfied by the plan process, such as productivity improvement, cost reduction, or market expansion.

Step two of the growth plan process is identification of the future marketplace events that are desired. The starting time of the events must be set. This step also requires quantifying the events and their impact on the objectives and output goals. This includes such items as customer account growth, transaction volume changes, staff requirements, and facilities changes. Also included is a description of employee and customer work station functions and a count of the units needed to support the marketplace events. The future event list also becomes an input statement of workload determination for development resources.

Step three of the growth plan process is conversion of the future marketplace events, their quantification, and their objectives into data processing system capacity and performance needs.

○ Transactions become messages.

○ Work stations become terminals.

○ Market events become processor and data storage resource needs.

○ New events become development resource demands.

Step four of the growth plan process is a review of the support functions needed to implement and achieve the desired data processing system results. At this point, the following questions are asked:

○ What are the necessary support functions?

○ When and how are they provided?

○ What are the desired results?

○ How do you know that they will be provided?

Step five concludes the growth plan process with an assessment of the results. The results are compared to the original business goals of the plan process. Actually this testing process is part of each step.

○ Do the quantitatively described market events achieve your business goals?

○ Does the system and development resource fall within your allotted time span and budget?

○ Is the support for implementation identified and adequate?

The growth plan process is designed to offer a 4- to 6-year view of the future. Thus, at an earlier point in time its results provide an understanding of future needs. This knowledge and insight can serve to improve the preparation and use of these vital data processing resources. Also, the growth plan process helps you to arrange a continuous and timely ordering of equipment for data processing. Timely actions are important. Timely actions help to reduce the lead times from the point when a decision is made about the need for a marketplace event to the time when the decision is implemented. Timely actions help you to live better with the resources available for development and equipment.

The presentation of the growth plan process in this book is aimed at the general manager or those not involved in data processing management. It provides a complete framework for action. The proposed planning process in this book is not meant to be a theory of organization or a text on management practices. It is intended as a guide for the general manager in situations requiring preparation of a long-range data processing plan. It is not unusual to experience a 4- to 6-year lead time for major facilities. However, with the growth plan process you can set your own time range. Your selected time frame needs to be based on your own lead time demands.

THE EXAMPLES USED IN THIS BOOK

The examples used in this book are meant to be helpful to managers generally. However, the specifics are based on examples from the use of on-line data processing systems in the banking industry. "On-line" means communications-connected data processing and computer-supported work stations. The reasons for using banking type examples are these:

- Banks are major users of data processing systems.
- Banking provides good examples of the growth plan process steps and guidelines.
- Banks have problems typical of labor-intensive businesses whose growth is services-based.
- Banks are subject to the same on-going inflation in wage and fringes as most labor-intensive businesses.
- Banks have increasingly complex business operations.
- Banks face a major capital expense in providing adequate business branches.
- Banks are fast-growing users of data processing functions, especially on-line systems.
- Most readers of this book use bank services and understand their operation.
- Banking offers a view of several new and innovative trends, including the use of communications, the acceptance and growth of customer-based self-service, and employee-actuated work stations with access to customer data bases.
- The banking industry has been the primary user to date of these planning process techniques.
- Discussions with persons in the banking industry show a pressing need for these planning techniques.

Early Implementors of the Plan Process

The first plan was completed several years ago. Since then the bank using it has completed three generations of the long-range plan. The plan process results have been reconfirmed and updated twice more at about 18-month intervals. Since the end of the first plan cycle, most of the plan process steps relating to numeric quantifications have been computerized. The plan "numbers" are now routinely prepared with the use of computer work station techniques. These techniques use market growth plans to exercise preset assumptions for key numeric quantification calculations. The numeric quantifications are required by the built-in resource computation models. Printed output notes identify which results are based on market or system input assumptions and which are based on calculations. Charts and tables are printed directly from the computer model. (Examples of suggested charts and tables are shown later.)

The first and subsequent finished plans involved a data processing management review which highlighted future marketplace events and their data processing needs. With support of the using department, the plan content was used to direct the activities of the data processing operating and development groups. The plan and the plan process has shown the bank management that they can set, track, and achieve a processing plan driven by data for future events. However, their experience shows that a good plan results only with the direct participation of key executives.

Later Implementors of the Plan Process

Since the growth plan process was initially developed, it has been applied to financial institutions in the United States and Western Europe, generally using the same pattern as described here. At all times a small plan process team has been used. At least one member of the plan team is a banker, whose role is to provide a sense of banking direction in the marketplace. The other members include data processing planning, marketing or branch planning, systems implementation planning, and plan process implementation.

In the opinion of these banking executives, data processing equipment can provide extraordinary services to the banking industry. The real secret is to know what needs to be achieved in your market, for your customers, and with your staffs. Then these needs must be expressed in terms of quantifiable events so that the data processing organization can deliver results. The growth plan process provides that guidance. It describes the users' future needs early enough in the plan to allow timely implementation of data processing.

REMEMBER

Enough for philosophical thoughts. Let's get on with the job at hand! And remember these Golden Rules as we proceed:

- Keep the plan simple!

- A long-range plan is only current until the next early update of the plan cycle.

- When in doubt, assume that current trends will continue.

- Use the next update of the plan cycle to revalidate the trends and to reconfirm the desired market events.

- If you have an option, produce a *quick* plan. Support it with a set of future numeric quantifications and result estimates. There will be time later to refine and to reconfirm the details and estimates.

- The plan results are informative. However, the introduction of the growth plan process, and its repetition at reasonable invervals, is the important message.

CHAPTER TWO

An Example

CHAPTER GOALS

Apply the growth plan process and demonstrate its end result.

Show the future event options that are available for market events.

Measure the impact of each future event option.

Offer a quick economic assessment of the selected future event options.

Review the system resources used to achieve the future event results.

START AT THE END

Let's start with the results of the growth plan process. An example of the future event results and the method that produces them shows the proposed growth plan process. Included will be a quantifying of the selected future market events. Also, this example reviews some of the end uses and values of this growth plan process. In that way, this example assists your understanding and use of the growth plan process as described in the later chapters.

THE CHALLENGE

You are a bank president. Growth is occurring in your retail customer base and branch bank teller usage. The retail area includes those customers served through the branch banks. This customer group is important to you, for it provides two-thirds of your lendable funds. However, the branches are two-thirds of the expenses of running the bank. To handle growth in the past, you built new retail branches. Also, you hired tellers for the new branches. The cost of building a new branch in the usual brick and mortar form is getting too expensive: an average new branch costs $500,000 to $1 million. Also, these buildings cannot be moved to new areas to respond to changing market growth and business needs.

You have asked the vice presidents for retail marketing and data processing planning to act as a planning team. You have asked them to answer the following sets of questions:

○ Assume that the retail branch account activity and market growth trends of the last 3 years will continue (call this the "current trend"): What will be the growth of accounts and branch teller activity over the next decade? Can the bank afford to respond to this growth in its usual manner?

○ What future market options are available to the bank (call these options the "future events")? If these future events or options change the branch system, how can the bank respond to these new growth patterns? When must these events start? How will they affect the need for more retail banking branches and staff?

You suggest that the planning team should construct its answer from current data and trends. If the answer shows a future action course, the estimates will be reviewed in depth later to confirm a detailed action plan. Also, the planning process results should confirm that the selected future events matched the goals and growth needs of the bank.

Current Trends

The current bank market results are known through the end of last year. Some key results are:

○ One million retail accounts, growing at 5 percent per annum for each of the last 4 years

○ Four branch transactions per month per account, growing at 4 percent per annum in each of the last 4 years

For the purpose of this quick planning process, a 10-year span has been selected as the time frame. Also, at least the preceding 3 years will be examined to set the current trend base. These years are as shown in table 2-1. If "last year" lacks complete

Table 2-1

YEAR	TIME PERIOD
Current	
-3	Three years ago
-2	Two years ago
-1	Last year
Future	
1	This year
2	Next year
3	Year ending 3
4	Year ending 4
5/6	Year ending 6
7/8	Year ending 8
9/10	Year ending 10

results (if it's too early in this year), feel free to shift your own report scale by one year and call it "this year." You could also estimate the end results for last year from the results for the partial year.

Growth of Customer Accounts

The number of customer accounts per branch is a clue to the expected branch revenue, deposits, and income. These key values and their trends are available from branch office records. Table 2-2 shows the expected current trends (operations that continue unchanged) for customer accounts. Result: A growth of over 60 percent (1.63/1.00) in retail accounts can be expected by the end of the next decade. This is based on expecting the current trend in growth to continue over the plan period.

Growth in Branch Usage for Customer Accounts

Branch usage may involve many types of transaction and staff persons, including tellers, managers, administrators, and others. The key usage is the teller transactions. Growth statistics are

Table 2-2

YEAR	CUSTOMER ACCOUNTS (K)*
Current	
-3	900
-2	950
-1	1,000
Future	
1	1,050
2	1,100
3	1,160
4	1,220
5/6	1,340
7/8	1,480
9/10	1,630

* "K" is abbreviated from "kilo," which means 1,000, as in "kilogram" and "kilometer."

used to show the expected growth in teller usage. Changes that increase the capacity of a branch to handle customer usage per teller are very desirable. Usually, increased teller usage must be matched by an increased output per staff member. Output per teller foretells the changes in branch expenses. Although growing usage output per teller means that branch expenses are growing more slowly than branch usage, that does not mean that the branch costs will be containable. Table 2–3 shows the expected teller output, based on the assumption that the current trends in transactions such as deposits and withdrawals will continue. Result: A growth of over 48 percent (5.92/4.00) in the branch transactions per account may be expected by the end of the next decade. This is the current trend.

Growth in Total Branch Usage Activity

Total branch usage is the product of account growth and usage per account. When we combine the key values from the previous table into table 2–4, we see the combined impact of this account growth and usage per account. Result: A growth of over 140 percent (9.65/4.00) in the total branch usage load may be expected by the end of the next decade.

Table 2–3

YEAR	CUSTOMER ACCOUNTS (K)	USAGE PER ACCOUNT PER MONTH
Current		
–3	900	3.70
–2	950	3.85
–1	1,000	4.00
Future		
1	1,050	4.16
2	1,100	4.33
3	1,160	4.50
4	1,220	4.68
5/6	1,340	5.06
7/8	1,480	5.47
9/10	1,630	5.92

Table 2-4

YEAR	CUSTOMER ACCOUNTS (K)	USAGE PER ACCOUNT PER MONTH	TOTAL BRANCH USAGE LOAD (K/MONTH)
		Current	
−3	900	3.70	3,330
−2	950	3.85	3,650
−1	1,000	4.00	4,000
		Future	
1	1,050	4.16	4,370
2	1,100	4.33	4,760
3	1,160	4.50	5,220
4	1,220	4.68	5,710
5/6	1,340	5.06	6,780
7/8	1,480	5.47	8,100
9/10	1,630	5.92	9,650

Growth in Branch Teller Output

Last year each teller handled an average of 5,000 branch transactions per month. However, the teller output also has been improving at a rate of 2 percent per annum. Table 2-5 shows the increase in teller output, based on current trends. Result: The 2 percent per annum teller output gain will provide a 22 percent

Table 2-5

YEAR	USAGE PER TELLER (K/MONTH)
	Current
−3	4.8
−2	4.9
−1	5.0
	Future
1	5.1
2	5.2
3	5.3
4	5.4
5/6	5.6
7/8	5.9
9/10	6.1

growth (6.1/5 = 1.22) over the next decade. This is less than the total branch usage growth of 140 percent for the same period.

Growth in Branch Teller Staff to Handle Usage

The number of tellers needed to satisfy the current trends can be computed. It is found by dividing the monthly branch usage or output volumes by the average usage volume handled by a teller per month. Table 2–6 shows the teller count needed to handle the branch usage, using values from the previous two tables. Result: There is a teller headcount increase of 98 percent (1,582/800 = 1.98) to handle a growth in branch usage of 140 percent (9.65/4.00 = 2.41). The usage came from an account growth of over 60 percent (1.63/1.00 = 1.63).

Teller wages and fringe benefits are estimated conservatively to be increasing at 7 percent per annum, which compounds to a projected 97 percent increase for the decade. This results in a growth in total teller wage expense of 290 percent (1.98 x 1.97 = 3.9) for the decade.

To the growth in the teller staff, we must add the growth in support staff. Also, added space will be required to house the increase in tellers, support staffs, and managers. These factors could add up to a set of going-out-of-business numbers. No bank

Table 2–6

YEAR	USAGE PER TELLER (K/MONTH)	TOTAL BRANCH USAGE LOAD (K/MONTH)	TELLER STAFF
		Current	
−3	4.8	3,330	694
−2	4.9	3,650	745
−1	5.0	4,000	800
		Future	
1	5.1	4,370	857
2	5.2	4,760	915
3	5.3	5,220	985
4	5.4	5,710	1,057
5/6	5.6	6,780	1,211
7/8	5.9	8,100	1,373
9/10	6.1	9,050	1,582

can absorb this rate of growth in expenses. Nor can the bank expect to pass these costs on to its customers in the form of fees or charges. This expense squeeze is hard to control, especially when interest rates and operating expenses are also high.

THE FUTURE EVENT OPTIONS

At this point your able planning team has reached their first key issue. The bank cannot afford to handle account and usage growth in a usual manner. Changes are needed to increase branch output. A quick survey of the banking industry indicates that several future options are available in the marketplace now. One or more of the options need to be quantified. A solution must be chosen and put into a marketing plan supported by data processing. Then the options need to be tested to assure that the right results are achieved. The first goal of the planning team is to handle the account and usage growth *without* any net growth in staff or conventional branches for the decade.

Option 1: Branch Teller Automation

In this future option, each teller is provided with a work station that gives direct access to each customer's data base. Use of these stations increases teller output by cutting transaction times. It also reduces manual entry such as data capture. It results in better control with less errors and less bad account losses. Each teller work station has a display screen, a keyboard, a bank card magnetic stripe reader, and a receipt printer.

WORK STATION INSTALLATION PLAN

A work station will be provided for each teller. It will take several years to install all the work stations and to achieve all of their planned output improvement. These installation factors and added output estimates will be as shown in table 2-7. The table indicates the rate at which new work stations will be installed. Also, it shows the rate at which teller output is expected to improve. Note that there is a limit to how much the new work stations help to improve teller output. Future trends like these

Table 2-7

YEAR	% TELLER STATIONS INSTALLED	% TELLER OUTPUT GAIN
1	0	0
2	10	10
3	30	15
4	50	20
5/6	90	25
7/8	100	25
9/10	100	25

can be projected from pilot tests or from the results of prior work station installations.

NEW TELLER OUTPUT RATE

New output gains are achieved by those tellers with access to the new work stations. The growing number of work stations installed results in growing output from the work stations. Thus, there is a projected increase in teller output. Table 2-8 shows the improved teller output over time. Also, it shows the increase in the number of available work stations over the plan period.

Result: The new teller output rate projection has been applied to those tellers with the work stations. The output of those tellers improves up to the projected teller output gain. Net teller output (for all tellers with work stations) has improved by 52 percent (7.6/5.0 = 1.52). However, this will not fully offset the total usage growth, which was projected to increase by 140 percent during the same period.

Table 2-8

YEAR	% TELLER STATIONS INSTALLED	% TELLER OUTPUT GAIN	IMPROVED OUTPUT PER TELLER (K/MONTH)
1	0	0	5.1
2	10	10	5.3
3	30	15	5.5
4	50	20	5.9
5/6	90	25	6.9
7/8	100	25	7.4
9/10	100	25	7.6

Let us apply the improved teller output rate to the projected workload. This results in a slower growth in the total teller staff. These changes are shown in table 2–9. Result: Use of the improved teller output rate reduces growth in teller staff in the future. (This may not mean that the branches and tellers are in the right locations: more on that issue later.) But there is still a large growth in tellers. The total teller count has increased by 61 percent (1,290/800 = 1.61) for the decade. This results in a 218 percent (1.6 x 1.97 = 3.18) projected increase in teller wage expense for the 10-year period.

Option 2: Automatic Teller Machines

These units offer self-service banking transactions. Customers receive a magnetic-striped plastic bank card. They also receive a personal identification number (PIN). The card and the PIN allow customers to perform account transactions, which include depositing funds, withdrawing funds, transferring funds, and making account inquiries. All of these are achieved without requiring the services of a teller. In fact, an automatic teller machine (ATM) electronic transaction also takes the place of the paper processed by a teller. An ATM is usable seven days a week and up to 24 hours a day.

It will take a few years to install all of the ATM units needed and also to achieve a growth in customer use of the ATMs. Thus

Table 2–9

YEAR	% TELLER STATIONS INSTALLED	% TELLER OUTPUT GAIN	IMPROVED OUTPUT PER TELLER (K/MONTH)	NEW TELLER STAFF	REDUCED TELLER STAFF
1	0	0	5.1	857	0
2	10	10	5.3	898	−17
3	30	15	5.5	949	−36
4	50	20	5.9	968	−89
5/6	90	25	6.9	983	−228
7/8	100	25	7.4	1,094	−279
9/10	100	25	7.6	1,290	−312

it will take time to achieve the projected decrease in the growth of teller usage (see table 2–10).

Assume that only 60 percent of ATM transactions replace teller use. The other 40 percent of ATM use is new or nonteller counter usage, such as new customer inquiries for account balance information. Assume that to be justified an ATM needs to achieve a rate of 5,000 teller transactions per month in its first year of use (equivalent to a human teller). Thus the ATM needs to handle a total of 8,300 transactions (5,000/60% = 8,300) per month. Further, assume that the volume of customer use of ATMs increases at 20 percent per annum. This builds ATM use to a maximum of about 16,000 teller-type transactions per month by the 10th year, out of a total volume of 27,000 transactions (16,200/60% = 27,000) per unit per month.

AUTOMATIC TELLER USAGE VOLUMES

The first step in determining future trends for automatic teller machines is to fix the number of units to be installed. The second step is to set the expected usage rate. Table 2–10 shows the start and growth of installed ATMs, then gives the expected ATM usage.

Result: The usage rate grows over an 8-year period of ATM use. Also, the number of units increases over a 6-year period. These are key values in estimating overall ATM usage. These values must be checked during each plan cycle. If changed, the table should show the most recent values. Note that this usage is

Table 2–10

YEAR	ATMs INSTALLED	TELLER-TYPE USAGE PER ATM UNIT (K/MONTH)	TOTAL ATM TELLER-TYPE USAGE (K/MONTH)
1	0	0	0
2	0	0	0
3	15	5.0	75
4	30	6.0	180
5/6	60	8.6	520
7/8	80	12.4	990
9/10	80	16.0 (max)	1,280

not the total ATM usage. It only shows the transactions that replace teller use.

TELLER SAVINGS
FROM AUTOMATIC TELLER MACHINES

As ATM usage increases it reduces the need for increase in the teller staff. These increases reflect only the ATM usage that replaces teller use. There is also ATM usage from new and added transactions due to the ATM's being available. Table 2-11 shows both types of increase in ATM usage. Result: There is a slowing of teller staff growth through the use of automatic teller machines. The table shows how much the need for teller staff growth is reduced through the use of the ATMs (1.28 million/ 7.6 K = 168).

However, there will be added expense for service personnel and system to support the ATM units. (More about those cost elements later.) The combined results of options 1 and 2 need to be examined in order to check the progress toward the study objective. Remember, the study objective was *no* staff growth over the decade.

Combined Options 1 and 2 Savings

Options 1 and 2 can be used together. Option 1 increases teller output. Option 2 transfers teller usage to ATM. Table 2-12 shows the results of applying both options. Note that the ATM savings start later, because ATM use starts later. The "output per teller" includes the teller usage moved to the ATM.

Result: Combining these two marketplace events has increased teller output by 76 percent (8.8/5.0 = 1.76). However, there is still a growth of 38 percent (1,102/800 = 1.38) in the number of tellers required to handle the account and transaction growth. The teller wage expense growth is projected at 172 percent (1.38 x 1.97 = 2.72). As used before, 1.97 is the expected teller wage growth for a decade.

These results also require more growth in the supporting staffs and working space. Assume an average of 7 tellers (and other staff) per branch office. The reduced staff need for 480 tellers (1,582 − 1,102 = 480) would avoid the need to construct

Table 2-11

YEAR	ATMs INSTALLED	TELLER-TYPE USAGE PER ATM UNIT (K/MONTH)	TOTAL ATM TELLER-TYPE USAGE (K/MONTH)	IMPROVED OUTPUT PER TELLER (K/MONTH)	REDUCED TELLER STAFF BY ATMs
1	0	0	0	5.1	0
2	0	0	0	5.3	0
3	15	5.0	75	5.5	−15
4	30	6.0	180	5.9	−31
5/6	60	8.6	520	6.9	−75
7/8	80	12.4	990	7.4	−134
9/10	80	16.0 (max)	1,280	7.6	−168

Table 2-12

YEAR	UNIMPROVED TELLER STAFF	REDUCED STAFF BY TELLER AUTOMATION	REDUCED STAFF BY ATMs	NEW TELLER STAFF	BRANCH USAGE PER TELLER (K/TELLER)
−1	800	0	0	800	5.0 (4,000K/800)
1	857	0	0	857	
2	915	−17	0	898	
3	985	−36	−15	934	
4	1,057	−89	−31	937	
5/6	1,211	−228	−75	908	
7/8	1,373	−279	−134	960	
9/10	1,582	−312	−168	1,102	8.8 (9,650K/1,102)

69 more branch offices (480/7 = 69). At a half million dollars per branch, that avoids a capital investment of almost 35 million dollars—if the needed land could be found. However, the plan objective of *no staff growth* has yet to be achieved.

So let us look at another future option.

Option 3: Automated Branch Office

The automated branch office requires less staff and building expense. It uses around-the-clock automatic teller machines for routine transactions. It uses a small staff during office hours for other business. This staff is used to open accounts and to accept loan requests. This type of branch is much less expensive to construct. It may be moved at lower cost to other locations. It may be put in a shopping mall, a school campus, a factory, or a building lobby.

These units house one or two automatic teller machines to provide teller-type usage. The automatic teller machines have the same teller usage output factors as shown previously for option 2. The teller-type usage does not show the new and added usage from the ATM use. Table 2–13 shows the total use for the automated branch during the plan period.

TELLER STAFF SAVINGS
FROM THE AUTOMATED BRANCH OFFICE

This plan needs a period of four years to develop, test, and start the use of these new facilities. Table 2–14 shows the sav-

Table 2–13

YEAR	AUTOBRANCH ATM COUNT	TELLER–TYPE USAGE (K/MONTH)	TOTAL AUTOBRANCH ATM USAGE (K/MONTH)
1	0	0.0	0
2	0	0.0	0
3	0	0.0	0
4	20	5.0	100
5/6	60	7.2	430
7/8	80	10.4	830
9/10	100	14.9	1,490

Table 2-14

YEAR	AUTOBRANCH ATM COUNT	TELLER-TYPE USAGE (K/MONTH)	TOTAL AUTOBRANCH ATM USAGE (K/MONTH)	OUTPUT PER TELLER (K/MONTH)	REDUCED TELLER STAFF
1	0	0.0	0	0.0	0
2	0	0.0	0	0.0	0
3	0	0.0	0	0.0	0
4	20	5.0	100	5.9	−17
5/6	60	7.2	430	6.9	−62
7/8	80	10.4	830	7.4	−112
9/10	100	14.9	1,490	7.6	−196

ings in teller staff. These savings result from using this new type of branch to handle marketplace growth. The estimate of output per teller is from the option 1 data used previously. The estimate of teller-type usage per ATM is from option 2 data used previously.

Result: These results are like those of option 2 with the use of the automatic teller machines. However, they are delayed because of the later starting time. The savings from option 3 may be gained at the same time as the savings from the other options. This is because savings from options 1 and 2 are from existing branches. The savings from option 3 are from new branches.

Combined Options 1, 2, and 3 Savings

Table 2–15 shows the impact of all three options. Result: Use of the three options still requires a growth of 16 percent (934/800) in teller staff. This teller staff peak occurs in year three of the plan. This is before the full savings impact of options 2 and 3. The combined savings in teller growth of all three options is 85 percent (1,582 −906/800). This is the direct result of slowed growth in the teller staff.

Results

The net impact of the three options is to slow the teller growth to 13 percent (906/800 = 1.13) for a decade. This is about a 1 percent per year growth, a very low rate of growth, and is probably smaller than the error of the estimating accuracy of these results. The low growth in teller staff was achieved by raising the effective teller staff output by 114 percent (10.4/5.0 = 2.14). This is a large savings. It offers a result that must be pursued. Further options may also improve branch teller output: improved teller education, less use of paper, and further expansion of self-service are a few of such options. In preparing an actual plan, a more complete list of options would be used. The present example was limited to three options to demonstrate more easily the plan process concepts and results.

Table 2-15

YEAR	UNIMPROVED TELLER STAFF	REDUCED STAFF BY TELLER AUTOMATION	REDUCED STAFF BY ATMs	REDUCED STAFF BY AUTOBRANCH ATMs	NEW TELLER STAFF	BRANCH USAGE PER TELLER (K/TELLER)
−1	800	0	0	0	800	5.0
1	857	0	0	0	857	
2	915	−17	0	0	898	
3	985	−36	−15	0	934	
4	1,057	−89	−31	−17	920	
5/6	1,211	−228	−75	−62	846	
7/8	1,373	−279	−134	−112	848	
9/10	1,582	−312	−168	−196	906	10.7

Table 2-16

| | FUTURE RESULT | EVENTS | | |
		PILOT	START	END
Option 1	Teller output	Year 1	Year 2	Year 7
Option 2	ATM	Year 2	Year 3	Year 8
Option 3	Automated branch	Year 3	Year 4	Year 10

FUTURE EVENT TIME MAP

A key need in any action plan is a specific list of the future marketplace events, including their timing, sequence, and relation to similar events. To show the concept of a time map, consider the three options shown before. These future options and their marketplace events are as shown in table 2-16.

The impact of these options has already been shown. A decision to proceed with these options requires work on the application and system development. Further, the start of these options requires a development plan as well as an installation plan to put the units into use, for the units must ultimately be used by customers. The units will also need the proper staff support and service.

The proposed percentage of work stations installed per year (to a total of 100 percent) is shown in table 2-17.

It is worthwhile to combine these data into a single time map, to show the marketplace events that are planned. Also, a similar map may be used to show the actual installation rates. However, it is also worthwhile to show total installations, as in table 2-18.

The future event time map is a way to show the new elements in the plan. It shows the planned marketplace events over the plan period. It is a key goal of the planning team to show these events. The plan must include the events and their timing sequence. The percentage of units installed may be combined into the same time map or may be shown in a separate table. In either

Table 2-17

| FUTURE RESULT | PLANNED % INSTALLATION RATE BY YEAR | | | | | | |
	1	2	3	4	5/6	7/8	9/10
Teller automation	0	10	20	20	20/20	10/0	0
ATM	0	0	19	19	19/19	10/5	0
Automated branch	0	0	0	20	20/20	10/10	10/10

Table 2–18

MARKETPLACE EVENTS	ACTUAL EVENTS AND TOTAL % INSTALLED BY PLAN YEAR						
	1	2	3	4	5/6	7/8	9/10
Teller automation	Pilot	Start				End	
		10%	30%	50%	90%	100%	100%
ATM	0	Pilot	Start			End	
			19%	38%	76%	100%	100%
Automated branch	0	0	Pilot	Start			End
				20%	60%	80%	100%

event, these data are needed to project and develop the resources required to install the new options.

With a plan process that repeats within a cycle of 18 to 24 months, other changes in later plan cycles will be needed to update and refine these time maps. Some events will begin on time or even early; others will be delayed. The net overall plan will, hopefully, balance out the early and late events, and the end result will be close to your plan needs. Updating in later plan cycles provides a fine tuning process for system changes. When development resources and installation capacity are developed and applied on a smooth and even basis, the system and capacity plan will more likely allow your future events to occur on schedule.

Yearly Future Event Project List

The future event time map shows the marketplace events as a sequence of related events for the future time frame. A valuable set of data is obtained by categorizing all of the entries from the time maps by the year when the event occurs. The input to the categories is drawn from all areas from which events are derived. This process gives a yearly project list for future events. The list shows the new event starting date workload for each year.

Let us use the future event time map as an example. We obtain the following future event project list:

Year 1
    Teller output pilot

Year 2
    ATM pilot
    Teller output installation started

Year 3
    Automated branch pilot
    ATM installation started
    Large increase in teller work station installations

Year 4
    Automated branch installation started

Year 7/8
    Teller output completed
    ATM installation completed

Year 9/10
    Automated branch installation completed

This list gives a basis for assigning total manpower and budget dollars in a plan for data processing action. Project time frames may extend for a long period, especially if the projects contain major construction of space. A yearly list of future event projects provides an early opportunity to see the total work load. The list gives a basis for adjusting schedules. Following the plan, steps may be taken to combine projects, also, other steps may be taken to conserve or optimize use of resources by adjusting the timing of events.

Number of Work Stations

The time map of future events shows the dates of major marketplace events. Also, the map shows the start, growth, and finish dates for initiating each key thrust. The same time frame may then be used to count the work stations, which is needed to achieve the set of future event targets, as shown in table 2–19.

Result: The work station count implies several important needs. First is the demand for installation designs and human support factors, as well as the electrical, carpentry, and other skills needed to make it all happen in a timely way. Note that raw counts by themselves can be misleading. For example, an

Table 2–19

YEAR	TELLER WORK STATIONS	ATMs	AUTOMATED BRANCHES	TOTAL WORK STATIONS
1	Pilot	0	0	0
2	90 Start	Pilot	0	90
3	280	15 Start	Pilot	295
4	460	30	20 Start	510
5/6	761	60	60	881
7/8	848	80	80	1,008
9/10	906	80	100	1,086

automatic teller machine may be installed through the outer wall of a bank building, and that requires zoning permission, physical design, piercing heavy walls, hoisting a heavy safe, providing alarm interfaces, and several other related tasks. Hence, the difference in work station counts may not show the true work load. In either case, the installation projection is a useful tool to the support groups involved. It gives an early indication of the amount and extent of the effort. It provides managers with a tool for allocating resources and establishing schedules.

A QUICK ECONOMIC ASSESSMENT

My intent is to leave the detailed economic studies to the specific projects that follow from these plans. However, it is necessary to test the plan now in order to show that the plan is within reason and capable of reaching its goals. Economic testing is needed several times during the plan process to avoid a delayed surprise at the end of the planning process.

In this example, a quick economic assessment is required. The assessment examines cost factors, cost avoidance, and enlarged marketplace value versus the expense of planned improvements, as follows:

Cost Avoidance

Slowed teller growth $(1,582 - 906 = 676)$
$676 \times \$15 \, K = \$10.1$ million ($\$15 \, K$ wages/teller)

Branch construction avoidance (676/7 = 97)
(One branch saved per seven tellers)
97 x $500 K = $48.5 million ($500 K cost/branch)

Total = $10.1 million + $48.5 million = $58.6 million

Automation Expense

Teller automation [906 × ($5 K + $5 K)]
($5 K work station, $5 K network attach)
906 x $10 K = $9.1 million

ATMs (100 + 80) x ($25 K + $25 K + $5 K)
($25 K/ATM, $25 K installation, $5 K network attach)
180 x $55 K = $9.9 million

Automated branches (50 x $200 K)
50 x $200 K = $10.0 million

Data processing expense (906 + 180 + 50) x ($10 K/work station)
1,136 x $10 K = $11.4 million

Total = $9.1 million + $9.9 million + $10.0 million + $11.4 million = $40.4 million

From the point of view of a quick review, this analysis indicates a cost avoidance that is 45 percent greater than the anticipated expense ($58.6 M/$40.4 M = 1.45). However, several factors were *not* included: inflation, other staffs and support personnel, and the costs or benefits of a supporting bank card plan (which is already being used). Other factors not included are possible price changes in data processing, the cost of development, and installation support needs. Also, there are marketplace benefits from an aggressive and modern marketplace stance. These results give added support to the proposed action plan. At this point it is necessary to examine the system resource needs before estimating an overall result.

Buying Output Results
with Data Processing Function

The conclusion is that the use the future options has "purchased" added output results. This added output was shown in terms of slowed teller growth. The example, as shown in the quick economic study, had the following results:

Expense of teller growth (simple example)
Teller salary $15 K/year
Prorated branch costs $7 K/ year
Total expense/teller $22 K/year

Prorated data processing costs to reduce growth of teller staff
Automation expense $40.4 M/4 years
Reduced growth of teller staff   676 tellers
Expense/reduced growth $14.9 K/year

The net result is that using data processing for automation has increased branch output. The added output was acquired at $14.9 K per person of avoided increase in teller staff. This is a 48 percent return on the cost of equipment used to slow the growth in teller staff ($22 K/$14.9 K = 1.48). Had the future options not been pursued, an added growth count of 676 tellers would be needed over the decade. This would have cost, in today's expense terms, $14.9 million (676 x $22 K/year).

SYSTEM RESOURCES

The marketplace event plan, together with its key numerically quantified values, provides an input to a system resource analysis. The growth in customer accounts and branch related usage will be handled with the equipment provided by the three future options. How do those future options relate to the system's resources?

Work Stations Become Terminals

A teller work station consists of four terminal units: display, keyboard, magnetic stripe bank card reader, and receipt printer. These units are coordinated by a branch controller with a terminal, at the rate of 10 work stations to a controller. Therefore each work station represents 4.1 terminals. The entire terminal count grows as shown in table 2–20.

Table 2-20

YEAR	TELLER WORK STATIONS	TERMINALS	ATMs	TOTAL COUNT OF TERMINALS
1	0	0	0	0
2	90	369	0	369
3	280	1,148	15	1,163
4	460	1,886	50	1,936
5/6	761	3,120	120	3,240
7/8	848	3,477	160	3,637
9/10	906	3,715	180	3,895

This work station count provides a view of future needs for equipment purchases. It also shows the need for system support and installation support. Also needed to support these units is a communications network, data processing facilities, and storage for customer records and transactions.

Converting Teller Usage to Messages

A teller transaction, such as cashing a check, requires several messages in an electronic banking environment. The first message is to the controlling computer and data base to request approval or enough data to make a local decision. The second message, to the work station, is to give the decision or to provide data for a local decision. The third message, to the controlling computer, is to confirm the transaction completion and also, if needed, to provide data for record updating, journaling, and other bookkeeping functions. This third message is not under the same time pressure as the others. Hence, third messages may be grouped with the next first message so that a message may include portions of two transactions for communication purposes. This gives an average of 2.5 messages for each transaction handled through the teller automation equipment. See table 2-21.

Converting ATM Usage to Messages

The automatic teller machines usually use a three-message network process. In addition, when we first considered the teller-related benefits from the use of the automatic teller machines,

Table 2–21

YEAR	BRANCH TRANSACTIONS (K/MONTH)	% TELLER WORK STATIONS INSTALLED	TELLER MESSAGES (K/MONTH)
1	0	0	0
2	4,760	10	1,200
3	5,220	30	3,900
4	5,710	50	7,100
5/6	6,780	90	15,300
7/8	8,100	100	20,300
9/10	9,650	100	24,100

only 60 percent of the transactions were counted. The remaining 40 percent are new transactions, such as inquiries that do not relate to the previous teller branch usage. However, they do need network handling. Therefore, network message loads for the automatic teller machine need to be increased to a full 100 percent of the ATM usage. This is 1.67 × the prior teller-related transaction usage.

In table 2–22, ATM usage and automated branch usage are shown in columns (1) and (2) and totaled in column (3). The total usage in column (3) is multiplied by 1.67 and shown as total ATM in column (4). This converts from teller-type ATM transactions to total ATM transactions. The latter total reflects new ATM transactions, such as customer inquiries. The total transactions are multiplied by 3.0 messages per transaction to give the total message count in column (5).

Arrival Rates Become Processing Loads

The previous table shows a large growth in message volumes. However, these volumes cover an entire month. To be meaningful in network terms, the message volumes need to be expressed as a volume count per second. This is required to convert them into network and processor usage. The teller automation equipment is used during branch business hours. This is 21 days × 6 hours × 3,600 seconds, or .45 million seconds per month. The automatic teller machines operate over a longer time period. This is 30 days × 20 hours × 3,600 seconds or 2.16 million seconds per month.

Table 2-22

YEAR	(1) TOTAL ATM TELLER-TYPE USAGE (K/MONTH)	(2) TOTAL AUTOBRANCH TELLER-TYPE USAGE (K/MONTH)	(3) TOTAL TELLER-TYPE USAGE (K/MONTH)	(4) TOTAL ATM TRANSACTIONS (K/MONTH)	(5) ATM MESSAGES (K/MONTH)
1	0	0	0	0	0
2	0	0	0	0	0
3	75	0	75	125	375
4	180	100	280	468	1,404
5/6	520	430	950	1,587	4,760
7/8	990	830	1,820	3,039	9,118
9/10	1,280	1,490	2,770	4,626	13,878

Table 2-23

YEAR	TELLER MESSAGES (K/MONTH)	TELLER MESSAGE ARRIVAL RATE (PER SECOND)	ATM MESSAGES (K/MONTH)	ATM MESSAGE ARRIVAL RATE (PER SECOND)	TOTAL MESSAGE ARRIVAL RATE (PER SECOND)
1	0	0	0	0	0
2	1,200	2.7	0	0	2.7
3	3,900	8.7	375	0.2	8.9
4	7,100	15.8	1,404	0.6	16.4
5/6	15,300	34.0	4,760	2.2	36.2
7/8	20,300	45.1	9,118	4.2	49.3
9/10	24,100	53.6	13,878	6.4	60.0

In table 2–23 the monthly teller message rate is in column (1). This is converted to a message per second rate in column (2) by dividing column (1) by .45. The monthly ATM message rate is in column (3). This is converted to a message per second rate in column (4) by dividing column (3) by 2.16. The total message arrival rates from columns (2) and (4) are added in column (5).

Table 2–23 shows average arrival rates. In network design it is necessary to provide for peak arrival rates. These could be several times larger than those shown in the table. The other factor to observe is the big difference between the arrival rates for teller and ATM. The extended hours of ATM usage helps to reduce the ATM arrival rate. The teller usage occurs in a shorter time period. Thus, one of the results of a change to electronic banking is this shift in network activity into periods outside of usual branch banking hours. More of this shift will occur as new remote banking functions are offered.

Estimating Processor Capacity

In this example the arrival rate data relate only to the electronic banking usage. There are many other tasks for the processing units. Included are the paper oriented and batch processing tasks, the program development workload, the other network and terminal support, and spare capacity for backup and unplanned needs. In this example we look only at the support needs for future events.

It is necessary to convert message arrival rates to a processing load. This requires an estimate of the number of processing instructions performed, on the average, for each arriving message. Assume that each message needs an execution of 10 K instructions. The message arrival table shows that the arrival rates vary. They range from a low of 2.7 per second to a 10-year growth to 60 messages per second during branch banking hours. This is a total of 60 x 10 K or 600 KIPs (thousands of instruction executions per second). That is not a large amount. However, we will wait until the total processor load is estimated to put this into context. The 600 KIPs result is enough to estimate the system resources needed for this task.

Estimating Data Storage Capacity

The prime need for data storage will be for customer records in an on-line processing environment. These customer data need to be stored in a medium that performs fast enough for the arrival times and instruction performance rates just described. In addition, several generations of customer records are needed at one time. Storage allows copies of the customer data to be sent to protected areas for safeguarding and security reasons. In this example the number of customer accounts ranges from 1.0 to 1.63 million over the 10 years of account growth. Your data processing systems department has a set of factors to turn number of accounts into data storage requirements. For example, each record needs 5,000 characters of data. Also, there are three copies of each record for security and backup. Therefore, the peak need is 1.63 million records x 5,000 characters x 3 copies. This total is 25 billion (thousand million or KM) characters. However, only one-third of that storage needs to be reachable by the electronic banking system. That size is well within the capacity of the data storage units to provide. A total capacity and storage management plan is needed. This includes storage for other processing, development, and back-up needs. This need for 25 KM (billion) character storage is enough to estimate the data storage resource for this task.

THE REPORT

At the beginning of this example you (as bank president) requested that the planning team return with a preliminary answer. This example shows the major steps in selecting and using future marketplace events. Also, the example helps to understand system resource needs. Beyond the points covered in the preceding discussion, there are other needs, such as development expense, marketing, project management, and supporting staffs. Also, a supply of plastic bank cards is needed for the self-service banking units. The bank cards must be marketed, produced, delivered, and otherwise administered.

Customers need personal identification numbers (PINs) to use the ATM units.

There will be other revenue flow from the bank cards depending on the type of card issued (credit, debit, or proprietary ATM access card). All-in-all, marketplace growth demands an early decision to select and proceed with the future event options.

The report to you, esteemed president of the bank, is as follows:

○ There will be growth of our retail branch banking business over the next decade. This growth will result in a large increase in staff and related expenses unless we implement a set of improvements in branch staff output.

○ There are a set of future events producing increased output that are worth considering in more detail. The future event option results appear to be cost justified. These events appear consistent with our need to project a modern banking image.

○ Taking advantage of the improved output options requires an electronic banking environment, which is a communications-based data processing system. These options also require application development resources and a few pilot efforts or test installations. Following development and testing, a work station installation effort will be needed.

○ The data processing action plan must be supported by a marketing effort. The action plan will include related improvement options, such as an electronic banking marketing effort, branch staff education, bank card marketing, and related actions.

Let's go! The next step is the new project plans. But more on that in a later step in the plan.

CHAPTER THREE

Step 1:
Setting Objectives

CHAPTER GOALS

Identify the objectives of the planning process.

Specify the time frames.

Select the business areas for the planning process.

PRINCIPLES IN THE EXAMPLE

Select a Key Part of the Business

The branch banking system is the source for two-thirds of the deposits (lendable funds) of the bank. However, the branches also account for two-thirds of the expenses of running the bank. These two numeric measures provide a high degree of proof that this is, indeed, a key part of the business. In other businesses it is important to seek out similar focal points of revenue and expenses as the starting point for a long-range planning process.

Select Major Market Challenges

The flow of funds from the branch banking system encourages marketplace competition for customer accounts and transactions. In fact, the competitors are not only banks: other industries offer both money investment opportunities and bank related services.

Seek Productivity Improvement Opportunities

The current growth trend for branch activity with accounts and transactions is up. If branch and teller capacity are expanded in proportion to this growth, then a bank incurs an impossible expense increase. In fact, it is a problem of a compound growth rate. The activity will double over a decade, and the employee wage expense will double over a decade. This will increase the total branch expense by a factor of four. In addition, the growth of supporting staffs and the increase in space to house them will also be an added expense. A bank needs an improvement option that reverses this increase in expenses while coping with the growing workload. Hence, the area to be focused on is an attractive longer-range planning opportunity for improving branch output.

Select an Industry Trend
to Improvement or Change

The area identified in the example—the evolution of the branch banking automation—involves several improvement options, all of which are being explored by the banking industry. In this particular case, the improvement options have been reported in the trade press; the reports have described several early tests and installations by other banks. Also, these activities have been confirmed by presentations at industry conventions, articles in trade papers, and actual installations. Selecting options with that degree of confirmation is an important objective for planning.

Seek an Evolutionary Scenario

The available options examined were evolutionary changes from the current branch structure. Some improvements were made at existing branches. The other improvement was a logical extension of a new concept of a less capital-demanding branch. This automated branch needs to be proved acceptable to the customer of a conventional branch.

Select Numeric Measures

The output of tellers in terms of transactions and account activity during a specified period is a well-established characteristic in the industry. Also, the assessment of the account capacity of a branch organization is well understood. Such numeric characteristics represent accepted and understood measures for assessing improvements. Thus the potential improvements offer a direct means to assess the investments required and the return expected.

Go for Testable Results

The improvement options examined lend themselves to pilot testing or early installation. Improvements of this nature allow an early setting of numeric values for results and an early way to introduce the changes into branch structure evolution. Part of this step of objective selection is the consideration of employees' reaction and how to communicate their role in the planning process. For example, the operation period for automatic teller machines extends into the nights and weekends. A reasonable test could validate this period of extended customer use. In most cases the bulk of bank employees lack interest in working during those extended times. Thus, the test results could be used by bank management to communicate to employees the nature of the extended operating hours that will be covered by the automatic teller machines.

Choose New Data Processing Capabilities That Are Available

The improvement areas examined in the example relied on new functional capabilities being provided to tellers by means of work stations in an on-line data processing environment. These are well-developed techniques that have already been installed at other financial institutions. Thus the improvement options being considered are real and represent realistic capabilities for the data processing system. However, this is not always the case, and this characteristic should be included as a planning objective.

Use Data Processing Development Resource Capabilities

Stay within the capacity of available resources for development. The improvements selected in this example were based on data processing techniques already in use. The existing system provided customer records, processed checks against the records, provided statements, and answered customer inquiries. Thus the proposed improvements were a logical extension of current activities; they were within the skills and scope of the application development resources. The on-line, communications-based nature of the system design may involve new skills. If so, the plan would require vendor support to educate the system development personnel and to provide appropriate design and development tools.

Ensure That Economic Assessment Is Feasible and Favorable

The improvement options represent, with their numeric measures, areas whose performance could be assessed. The improvements in the example offered a choice of continued unimproved operation versus an improved operation. It is always desirable to proceed with a choice of an objective that lends itself to this type of result. The result should produce a sufficiently large return to allow for a reasonable safety factor.

GENERAL OBJECTIVES

In the previous review (chapter 1) of the overall objectives for a longer-range data processing planning process, several general objectives were discussed. One of these was to seek a reduction in marketplace action constraints, that is, to seek the ability to make a marketplace decision to improve service for customers and then to be able to implement this decision within a reasonable time.

A second general objective was to develop the data processing system to be more effective. Effective development of the data processing system involves the use of budgets, available skilled people, and equipment to achieve specified objectives. If future objectives can be projected, then the data processing budgets, people needs, and equipment needs can be managed in a timely and controlled manner. If so, a key objective of the long-range data processing plans has been achieved. This planning objective is to provide the necessary future plan content to achieve that end result.

A third general objective previously identified was the use of the results of the long-range plan as a management tool. This use includes communicating to all management, to the data processing using departments (the users), and to the data processing providing departments the information about choices made for development of the future data processing capabilities.

A fourth objective is the use of the long-range plan as a bridge of understanding between the users and the data processing personnel. Joint preparation of plans helps both parties to communicate their requirements and responses and thereby aids in assuring better joint actions.

SPECIFIC OBJECTIVES

Beyond these general objectives there is a need to consider specific planning objectives that tailor the general objectives to fit the individual needs of your organization.

A PREDICTABLE SUBJECT FOR PLANNING

Start with two subjects for planning. The first specific objective should be to identify as an initial subject for planning a business area that is a reasonably known entity. The area selected should have needs, responses, and numeric measures that are routine and predictable. In the example, the planning objective was to assess branch operations. This area represents an evolutionary improvement in the marketplace interface with customers and involves a routine and predictable set of events. Moreover, the options for changes provide significant results in the form of improved output. Similar areas are evident in other industries, such as customer interfaces for manufacturing and other service type organizations. In any event, dealing with a routine and predictable set of events is a sound approach. It is the best type of subject for establishing the planning process as an acceptable and understandable management tool.

A NEW SUBJECT FOR PLANNING

Usually when the first specific objective is the selection of a predictable subject, it is easier to understand and implement the planning process in its first use. The second specific objective is the identification of a new and perhaps less predictable planning subject. The reason for picking this kind of subject in the second specific objective is that such a subject provides an opportunity to test the capacity of the planning process to project the solution to a new problem. A subject with an increased degree of uncertainty and with unknown elements requires a cyclical process. In the early stages, there is more skilled guessing. In the later stages, plans are refined and updated to reflect actual learning experiences in the development process. A case in point is the use of an automatic banking facility in which all transactions are handled independently of the tellers. This approach requires a good deal of cooperation between all the players—customers, branch banking department, data processors, and management. This improvement is a greater departure from a conventional branch, where customers are conditioned to dealing with the tellers. However, this improvement represents a more significant output improvement opportunity at the branch level. It also further reduces the capital requirements to reach retail banking customers.

Pilot Tests

This second type of planning subject, to be improved successfully, needs support by persons with important skills and know-how. This subject would benefit from an early pilot installation of one or several automated branches. This pilot effort would need to be closely supported by both user and marketing departments. There is a need for an introductory campaign to achieve customer and employee acceptance, which would be demonstrated through their use of these facilities. Since this is a new area, other support services would be needed, such as bank card distribution and facilities design.

New Business Areas

There is a wide variety of new areas that can serve as subjects for planning. The use of remote or communications-based services for remote banking at home or in a place of employment is a likely subject. Another is the automation of key organizational activities where they interface with your customer set, for example, marketing via interactive television such as videotex. A third area is that of customers' interface with industrial product design specifications via a remote but interactive data processing facility. Direct customer access is provided to specifications, dates, prices, and inventory control status, which are provided by an on-line, interactive work station. This is the wave of the future for self-service with speed, economy, and direct service.

A good example of remote function is the corporate cash management service offered by a number of banks. In this operation, the corporate treasurer has direct work station access to his data base in the data processing facility at the bank. The bank has collected, through a network service, the total cash position of a geographically distributed corporation. The bank provides mathematical models and analytical tools to assess the cash flow and position. It also provides a means for issuing instructions for cash moving or cash borrowing electronically.

These examples represent the second type of subject, the new business opportunity. This subject provides a new and untried objective for a longer-range planning process and for a focus on the development issues involved. (In a later section we discuss the need to show these future events with the evolution of current events.)

Focus on Labor-Intensive or Time-Intensive Activities

The planning process objective is to find these subjects. Historically, output improvement opportunities have been associated with labor-intensive and time-intensive activities. Within your organization, such activities are generally well known. Also known are the operations that represent long or constraining lead times. These are operations in which a significant improvement could cut your costs or enhance your marketplace response. As a general characteristic, these areas have a measurable numeric feature. This measurable feature shows how the cost-intensive activity will change in time. The changes occur as the future marketplace events in the plan take place. The use of current (unimpacted) and future (impacted) analyses of the future plan events provides a valuable numeric analysis of the results from the improvement options available. This also provides a basis for the quick economic assessment process that was demonstrated in the example.

Numeric Quantifying

Another important use of numeric quantifying is that the related future events lend themselves to establishing trends and measuring the success of efforts. This gives the participants an important management tool to determine if they are performing according to plan. It helps the planning process and plan recycling process by allowing a comparison of the current status and the probable results of future events.

Encourage User and Data Processing Plan Cooperation

The specific planning objectives should involve as a subject an area that is a reasonable extension of current data processing activities. Likewise, the subject for planning should be a reasonable growth area for the using department. By picking subjects or study objectives that have this combination of characteristics, the planning process encourages communications between the two activity focuses—data processing and the user department. Such subjects need to represent reasonable objectives that are both individual and collective.

An additional characteristic encourages cooperation between these two parties: this is the selection of user-identified numeric objectives associated with the planning objectives. This requires direct communication between the using and data processing providing groups regarding a common base for numeric measurement. It allows the data processing providing group to respond and to support achievement of the numeric goals. Both groups have a clear understanding of the measures of success and progress that they are collectively achieving.

Use Available Expertise

The plan objectives should be selected so as to be within the expertise of the available manpower. It is not practical to pursue a new objective for which expertise is not available or can not be internally generated. Some objectives are a logical extension of current experience for which existing expertise can be used to build an adequate skill base. That really is one of the major objectives of a pilot effort, which is an early effort to get experience. For example, a pilot project associated with automatic teller machines might also be used to develop the skills of marketing, installation, and customer education. These are the skills required to support a major automatic teller machine installation and marketing program.

SELECTING BUSINESS AREAS

Identify Major Business Segments

The business areas selected for the longer-range data processing planning process should relate to major business segments or opportunities. These are characterized by a number of specific traits. First, the identified area may encompass a large subset of your existing or prospective customer base; thus any activity that is undertaken can attract a large set of customer-type users. This gives a larger multiplying factor to take advantage of an investment in an advanced data processing solution.

Second, the area to be selected should also be one with a large or potentially large business opportunity. This may be a new way of serving the marketplace, a new set of product or revenue opportunities, or a new way to interface with the marketplace. A third desirable characteristic is the presence of a large revenue flow or the potential for one. Fourth, the kind of area to examine is one that has a large or disproportionate part of the operating expense or overhead. The choice of branch automation had many of these attributes. A large customer set, a significant production of lendable funds, but also a large segment of the bank operating expense.

Major Investments

Additional areas worth examination are those requiring major investments. Is a major investment required in a branch, manufacturing facility, or administrative/processing facility? If so, then those are opportunities to explore an output improvement alternative supported by data processing. These types of techniques were shown in the example through the use of an automated branch bank based on an intensive self-service application.

Accelerated Growth

Another characteristic to address in an area to be planned is a fast or accelerated growth occurring in the marketplace or in response to the marketplace. The danger in not addressing this type of area at an early point is that paper-based and labor-intensive solutions might need to be applied at the last moment. Thus, the lack of a long-range plan prevents adequate preparation. The consequence is costly in both expense and lost responsiveness.

Critical Constraints

In some areas the "old" way may prevent any reasonable response to an opportunity. These areas have an increased dependency on order-to-delivery cycles. Also, communications and information flow is required to overcome serious time constraints from people, processes, or procedures. Changes in the old paper-based, manually intensive areas may be limited by your ability to hire, train, or retain enough responsive people. The labor costs may be also prohibitive. In all cases these areas represent a business segment that ought to be examined for improvement opportunities.

Build on a Functional Base

Starting a new area of data processing planning should make maximum use of existing know-how. A common application base, a common business activity, or a common system implementation each represents a valuable base on which to build. In the example, we chose market coverage for retail banking as the common base. The branch structure, the branch staffs, the branch transactions, the customer interface, and the types of accounts all had a base in common with the planned improvements. In that way, the improvements could focus on needs without having to build an entirely new activity base from which to work.

Several Years of Experience

It is desirable to select an area in which the organization has several years of experience. This provides a knowledge base on which to build projections and trend evaluations. The existing understanding of customers and their transactions provides a reasonable base for setting numeric descriptors and ensures a basis for measuring progress.

SETTING TIME FRAMES

Critical Lead Times

Getting started with a long-range planning process for data processing requires some reasonable grasp of the time required to accomplish specific but critical results. The lead time on facilities may be long, as we mentioned previously. In addition, a preparation period is necessary. It may require several years to specify and develop the needed application and system programs, designs, and procedures. Some of these efforts may be overlapped with the lead times for facilities. However, if the management approval process demands an explicit economic justification tied to numeric projections, then some of the planning efforts may need to precede and be added to the lead times for facilities.

In the example, had the three improvement projects *not* been committed, then the branch facilities might have required 50 percent more space to house the added teller staffs. In the next few decades the transition from a paper-based to an electronic-based transaction system may require both alternatives. Both may be needed to cover the same extended capacity ranges in the same period. In either event, a comprehensive long-range plan is needed to assess the situation and to decide on the critical path(s), as well as to pick the earliest date at which the critical management decisions must be made to accommodate the transition from paper to electronics.

Market Entry Support Is a Must

Entering into a new business area or mode requires that the industry trends support the migration plan. There are a number of industry information sources that can provide insights into the time frame of the leading industry implementers. Vendors and competitors can also provide valuable clues for the timetable to be expected in the innovative business areas. Why is this consideration important? It is generally impossible, unless you have unlimited resources, to acquire the skills and impetus to open a new market area by your own efforts alone. Many a correct decision to proceed, based on market readiness, has stumbled over the lack of knowledge about potential problem areas or how to respond to them. In addition, there is significant value in a parallel effort of several industry members to prepare and train their collective marketplace users simultaneously. The cost of these early efforts are high, but the leaders consider the lead time into the market to be worthwhile. In any event, a long-range planning process is a critical tool in preparing for this type of progressive effort.

Being a Pioneer

There is a significant difference between being a pioneer and being an early implementor in a marketplace. The latter category blends the advantages of being early with the safeguards of having the skills and know-how to proceed with reasonable risk. The approach to consider is to put your overall plan in place but to select a checkpoint or two in the process. These are the checkpoints at which the pioneering efforts of others are closely examined. At that point you can fine-tune your plans for the unexpected, reconfirm your goals and objectives, and then proceed in a lower-risk environment. The early implementor does have a significant opportunity to realize the early benefits at a reasonable risk.

Seek Evolutionary Change

Is the change being considered evolutionary or radical? If it is new and radical, then an adequate safety factor must be provided for early learning experiences. Are you dealing with an area accustomed to change, in which change is an inherent characteristic? Are the participants capable of moving with changes? In these cases, the time factor may be established with more certainty. However, an adequate safety factor is a must in order to handle unknowns. It does not hinder the timetable to put safety factors in the plan, if the plan is reviewed at appropriate checkpoints to reassess them.

PRACTICAL CONSIDERATIONS

The time used to finish the activities in step 1 of the planning process should not be long or time-consuming. This is so if the responsible planning group is at a high level of management, with a good range of user and data processing skills. Also, when they recognize the iterative nature of this planning process, then results may be expected in a manner of hours and days. When the results of this phase are completed, they require top management agreement and a decision to proceed to the next planning phase. Subsequent steps will help to test and refine these results.

Remember, our key objective is *not* to put these findings into concrete. Rather it is to let the subsequent phases guide the final view. In all cases documentation is needed. It should record the selections made, the reasons they were chosen, their underlying assumptions, their source, and the confidence level of the assumptions. These are all important items to be documented in a succinct form. This allows the subsequent plan cycles to revalidate and confirm or modify the plan. Also, to know what has changed—and how.

The documentation of step 1 may be kept separate from the

body of the plan. This allows limiting distribution of these considerations to a select group of the top management, those associated with establishing the "philosophical" direction of the marketplace events and the data processing usage of the organization. The step 1 considerations could be quite valuable to the wrong groups. Correspondingly, it may not be desirable to communicate these decisions to implementing groups. In fact, these issues may be distracting. The implementors need to focus on the plan details and what needs to be done.

CHAPTER FOUR

Step 2: Projecting Marketplace Events

CHAPTER GOALS

State current trends for the selected marketplace areas.

Select future event options and project their effect on the current trends.

Set the function and number of work stations.

Project the work station usage needed to achieve the future events.

Involve the data processing users in the choosing of future trends and action options.

Obtain management support for the projected future events.

LESSONS FROM THE EXAMPLE

Set a Base Case

Our example projects the current trends and future events in branch banking. The future events are changes and improvements in response to the growth in customer accounts and usage. In the example we projected a base case, that is, a case with no change in the current trends: we assumed that the current branch activity and growth trends would persist. We also assumed for the base case that the branch staff output would have a modest increase through the plan period. This results from a normal but modest improvement in staff output. Thus, the base case provides a "before" set of actions and their activity volumes. This "before" value is the base against which we measure the changes resulting from applying future event options to the branch banks. The "after" or future event case reflects the new total branch output, which is the output after use of the selected future event options.

Select the Options Based on Their Impact

We looked at three options for future events in the example. Each option involved a change in the branch staff output, estimated in terms of customer accounts and usage. These estimates allow two ways to improve the branch bank output. First, we can slow or avoid further staff growth, while handling an increase in customer accounts and usage. Second, we can maintain the account and usage capacity of the branch bank without replacing staff turnover. The choice of options depends upon customer growth demand in each branch. In most cases, one of the future event options will apply best to the goals of the bank as a whole. The selected option will be used to estimate the future event impact on the current trends.

Provide a Time Map of Future Events

In the example we showed a "time map," which laid out the sequence of future event options and when they occurred in time. This event timing map serves several useful roles. It shows the dates by which new options are to start. Dating events to the nearest year is generally adequate. This offers a view of the rate at which we can realize the improved output. The timing chart also allows for a shift of dates for starting options or the joining of like events. These changes in event dates are a key tool. They let us adjust the total work load needed to start the options chosen and hence are a key tool for resource conservation.

We can now see the total workload needed to start future events in a given period. We get the total by adding the workload for all events in that period from all time maps. This total picture is useful in estimating the demands on people resources and budgets (time and dollars). If we need to, we can shift, join, or drop events, so that we can live within resource limits. As we change the sequence of events, the time map offers a quick view of the selected or remaining action options.

Trade New Event Timing for Resources

We found that each new future event option had an impact on branch bank staffing or output. Also, that each event had a date that determined when and how much of a result would be achieved. Sometimes it is possible to get results at an earlier date if we use more system or development resources. The added results can be estimated as we advance the date. Of course, we have to take into account the costs of advancing each starting date.

More often a market event from a competitor forces an advance in an event start date. Whether by choice or force, the decision process is improved by having more data with which to look at the options open for action. Data about results versus resources for the selected options allows us to judge costs and benefits of various options. This allows an informed decision process and response.

Seek Early Data to Confirm Option Results

The time map shows some options with a pilot stage. The pilots are shown when early data is needed to confirm results or the resources needed to start new options or both. A pilot phase allows early results from tests, live measurements, fine tuning of plans, and a sampling of the resource support needed for each option. A pilot stage lets us test the planning factors we have used. Sometimes the pilot results differ greatly from the planning factors used. In that case the planning factors must be revised for use in the next plan cycle. In that event, a timely next plan or cycle revision—in 18 months to two years—will allow us to reflect the latest pilot test results. In some cases a pilot effort is not needed or not worth the added expense. In those cases, we may have other experiences to guide the new options directly without going through the pilot stage.

Test the Economics of Selected Options

Each option will, at some point, need a detailed proposal from vendor(s). The detailed proposals will offer a great deal of added data about costs, equipment, resources, and results. At earlier steps, such data is not available. However, a modest overall economic test is possible, although this test is only as valid as the strength of the planning factors used. In the example, overall savings and costs were estimated; the planning factors were listed; and the method of their use was shown. The result was an economic test giving a gross picture of the expected impact on staff, output, and facilities. The test compared the results with the gross costs of equipment, installation, and the system. If we use a reasonable safety factor, this method gives us an early economic test of the selected options.

STATE THE CURRENT TRENDS FOR EACH MARKET AREA

Current Trends

Current trends show the output results based on the customer and staff actions of today. These trends may provide for modest changes. Current trends include the use of any automation that is now in use, but do not include any planned future changes or options, which are shown as future events and options.

The example showed how we estimated the size of current trends and recorded them. Current trends offer a base from which we can measure future results. This base includes current work station usage. Changes in the current trend picture between plan cycles allow us to measure and update the results of actions taken. Thus, the current trend study taken in a later plan cycle shows the impact of prior future events.

Which Key Values Are Used to Show Current Trends?

The key values for showing current trends are those that concern customers and their actions. Also, the key values show the type and volume of products and services we perform or provide. Let us look at a variety of key values useful for showing current trends (table 4–1).

Current Trend Period and Usage

We measure key values over a period of time in order to set a basic or current trend. This period of time needs to cover at least 2 to 4 years of actual results. A simple annual average of the growth trend for that period is a good starting point. A review of this trend line in each 18- to 24-month plan cycle offers an easy way to confirm or change the base plan key values and their current trends.

Table 4 1

TREND AREA	KEY VALUES
Customers	Accounts, accounts by type, service users, product buyers, and contracts
Market coverage	Branches, staffs, agents, sales persons, brokers, and order clerks
Action volumes	Transactions, dollar volumes, orders, inquiries, quotes, counts, and contracts
Media usage	Plastic cards, accounts, paper/documents, checks, sales and payment vouchers and statements
Work areas	Stations, locations, counter places, input/output devices, and related work places
Usage periods	Time of day, averages, peaks (hour, day, week, month, and season), and related volumes

These key values for current trends are basic to any future plan. We use them to describe the actions and activities of the business. Also, they describe the product and service delivery by volumes and time. These key values translate directly into earnings flow and the expense of doing business. The key values show the output measures of market coverage and product delivery.

The key values are used in the following three ways:

○ To help choose the market areas and the products or services to be followed in the plan

○ To describe the selected market or business areas and their current trends, as described previously

○ To reflect changes resulting from the impact of future plans

Project Future Trends

The changes are caused by the use of selected action options for future events. We measure the changes in key values, because we selected action options from the base point of the current trends results. One way to start is to assume that the current trends will continue. Another way to start is to set the first date for each new market event: each new event date will need an estimate of its impact on the related key values.

How does the new event affect the key values? Estimate how each key value will change by making an expert guess or by analyzing actual results based on prior experience. You need to document these assumptions. These estimates are then applied to the current trends (added or subtracted, as needed). The net result is the total for all of the selected events or options. This total is the effect of the plan and the future event changes to the prior plan of action. The effects of the future event are measured against the current trends base.

With this planning process we review the estimates again in the next plan cycle, in about 18 to 24 months. This type of periodic review will confirm the future trends and their results or provide a basis for modification. In some cases we will have available pilot tests or early results, and we may then use these results to support or improve our estimates. In other cases, actual market results will change the current and future trend factors. In either case, be prepared to update the current trend factors by actual market results measured since the last plan. Also, each plan needs to refine the future trends according to the actual results to date. The methods used to set future trend values in an earlier plan are then used to update the trend values for the later plan.

Describe and Use the New Event Time Map

Earlier, we learned about and used the new event time map. The time map shows the sequence of new marketplace events for all selected business areas. Within each sequence the time map reflects a buildup of results, ranging from early pilot efforts through the end of work station installation. We intend to update the new event time maps during later planning cycle updates. The event time map updates include schedule changes, adding or dropping events, and changes in the business areas covered by the plan.

During each plan cycle we also have a chance to focus on the latest priority actions. For such priority actions or changes, we can prepare the new event time map to a greater level of detail. For instance, we can add more subevents. The time intervals may be shortened from yearly to quarterly during the early years of the plan. These changes give more detail in the early periods of the plan.

Sequence All Events by Year

The new event time map becomes a key input to the new estimate of work load. All events from all maps are put into one list in sequence of event starting date. This gives a picture, by year, of the required work load completion dates.

Each new event entry should list the related user group or time map business area. This provides a cross reference for plan control. These entries allow a related view of the event goals and resources by year. This is also useful for tracking current budget results and future budget demands.

The new event time map also helps to give us a view of the

work load for the total systems activity. These activities include all of the functions for management, support, development, and operations. We should prepare an activity work load estimate for each new event. We can now put together a system work load estimate for all time maps, sequenced by starting year. This gives us the work load details to be supported by the system resources. This data will be used in the next plan (step 3) to find the system resources and support needed for plan action.

From the list in yearly sequence, we do another type of fine-tuning of the plan work load. Shifting timetables or event targets, joining like projects, or changing targets are all trade-offs we can use to adjust work loads. Another way we can reduce work load is to seek other solutions. For example, we could buy application or system programs from others. Another option is to let the user department provide its own application programs. We can explore the use of new language tools or packages, which are used by nonprogrammers but produce direct program output. (More on these options in plan step 4.)

The yearly work load list is a useful tool if it is used early enough to give results in time to do something about what we find. Application programs cost a great deal to produce and take time to finish. These programs use people who are in scarce supply. In most cases, the time needed to produce these programs is the key factor delaying the timing of a marketplace event. Program production is what makes the delay between a decision to activate a marketplace event action and the results of a marketplace event. If we act early we leave ourselves more options. Less costly but time-consuming results can be used if we allow enough time. The best answer to this problem of work load versus resources is to prevent a problem early, rather than to buy a quick but costly solution later.

Try a Usage Model

Some new tasks are for areas without prior data processing usage or experiences. To estimate those future events, a way to state and to measure the work is needed. A "usage model" describes a new event in a way that allows this quantification. The usage model is used to show the new event content, as illustrated by table 4–2.

Table 4–2

ACTION AREA	MODEL CONTENT
Customers' records	Type, size, volume, and growth rate
Activity	Type, volume, peaks, and growth rate
Media	Type, volume, peaks, and growth rate (e.g., bank cards)
Staff	Type, number, time used, and growth rate
Activity per staff	Ratio by type and growth rate
Product output per staff	Ratio by type and growth rate
Customers per staff	Ratio by type and growth rate
Facilities per staff	Ratio by type, costs, and growth rate

With these data, the model may be used to measure the effort needed to cope with new events or a set of new events. The model is also the base case to which further changes may be applied or referred. We may express each change in the same type of model content terms. You can then compare the changes for their impact on the base model. This is the same approach we used in the example.

The usage model is used like a new event from the time map. The result of each change or new event becomes an input to the system resource and development work load steps later in the process.

Relate the New Event Time Map to the Key Values

Each entry in the new event time map has key values that apply to it. These values are important descriptors. We have discussed their use earlier (see page 59). Also, the example showed how we can use the key values to find the current results and the future trend effects. Changing these values, under various event options, also allows us to measure changes in key factors such as staff size and output.

These changes offer a tool that lets us pick what is best among a set of options. Also, we may test changes for their impact on the other options. What are some of the tests? Less staff, more output, less time, less paper, earlier use, and lower costs are only a few of the tests we may use to select from a set of options. As the final options are selected and tested, they also indicate the places at which the events need to take place. The selected options show the type of data—input and output—needed to perform the tasks as part of the new event. These data help you choose locations for the work station activity and the types of work station capabilities needed.

Set the Number and Usage of the Work Stations

Work stations are the devices through which the data processing system accepts input and delivers results. The work station user may be a staff person, a user department member, or a bank customer being communicated to directly as in the use of a self-service device. We can describe work stations simply: input, display, output, and media functions. Key questions are: Who uses the work station? Do users share the work station with others? How does the work station work capacity relate to the key values shown for this event? When will we start to use the work station? How fast will the work stations be put in place? The answers to these questions offer a basis for setting the number of work stations. These data also help to set the build-up or installation rates and the work station usage.

Work stations have an activity rate for each type of event. In some cases the rate depends on the speed of the staff person. In other cases the usage rate depends on how fast customers arrive at or use the work station. Some usage is further reduced because it is restricted only to a portion of the possible users; for example, an automatic teller machine is limited to customers with the right type of plastic card, further limited to plastic card holders who have asked for a secret or personal identification number (PIN), and still further limited to those who remember the number and are willing to go to the work station and use the unit.

It is not unusual for a work station to have a high rate of usage. Automatic teller machines may also have a high usage during their extended hours of service, depending upon where they are located.

The planning process requires that these usage rates be estimated, tested, and, if necessary, revised according to actual results. The usage rates used in the plan process need to be documented as to their source, their size, and the level of confidence in their values. We should choose a total number of work stations allowing for all usage activity and the growth rates in the future event plan.

Check the Total Number of Work Stations

The quantity of each work station type is set for each event by the process just described. A chart showing total work station count by year will provide you with a picture of overall work station needs. The annual total for all work stations needed shows the range of effort required to place and support the future event plan. Looking at the year-to-year changes in these totals, you can get an early view of the work station installation support staffs required over time. This table will be used in planning step 3 (chapter 5) to convert work station needs to terminal or input-output device needs. It will also help to set the system development and support resources needed to make the future plan happen.

Measure the Work Station Usage

Work station usage starts with event actions. Each event action includes a basic set of key values that show the usage, both in time and volume, of providing the actions and service or product efforts. To show these volume or usage measures, planners need to define a measuring base. Usage numbers can vary over a given period because of activity peaks and changes. Holidays and end of the week, month, or quarterly periods all add to a broad range of volumes referring to the same event. Hence, you need a consistent measurement base. Let us use the total average monthly volumes. We need also the peak-to-average volume ratios for the most demanding time period of the year. This top demand period usually lasts only for a few hours, at most. It usually happens during a preholiday period. However, once measured, it offers an important system and network design input that will be needed later.

Document the Work Station Usage

You need to record the volume and times when the work stations are used, including the source of the estimates. Also, show other factors such as work hours per day, days per week, and weeks per month and year. Include the hours of usage per week. Enough data is needed to compute usage per second. This will be used later in fixing network and system resource at usage-per-second rates. Good records of these data enable you to compare changes in these measures in later planning cycles. This gives a basis for checking usage trends and growth. These usage volumes are also a basic factor for measuring plan results versus marketplace event goals.

Other Usage Factors

Events take place at widely scattered times during the business day. Some things happen during branch hours, some at night, other events take place around the clock and on most days of the week. In each case, the peak volumes and the period during which they occur may vary between events. In setting system resources, you should know the timing of peak events. If the peak events do not overlap, then you may need fewer total system resources. In fact, some future banking events, such as remote banking, will shift system usage to evenings and weekends. These time-shifted events reduce usage of the branches during daily branch hours. Thus, a good record of the active time periods is useful in this and future planning cycles. This record allows a careful review of the demand changes and how they vary between planning cycles.

OTHER FACTORS TO REVIEW

Geography

A number of marketplace actions take place across a broad geographic area. This fact increases in importance as mergers increase the area covered by individual banks and firms. Also, we can foresee a lowering of barriers to further spreading; for example, ending the ban on interstate banking will allow branch banks to cover larger areas. Coping with data processing needs for large geographic areas may be achieved by using a regional or local area data processing center. Within the region a central or shared function will support local needs. In a related way, other factors will increase the value of considering shared structure and response in a local area. These factors include travel time and expense. Also, it will be less costly to transport material to a local region. The costs associated with providing short response times will go down in an operation that is geographically closer or shared.

Options That Respond to Shared Area Coverage Needs

Several options help you to respond to local or regional needs in a plan for shared area coverage. A local handling center with its functions shared by several branches combines economy of scale with efficient use of resources. Use of distributed data processing or paper-to-electronic units on a shared basis is another option. For each type of shared marketplace action, we need to capture a set of key values. What are the related values and time factors? Is there enough activity to support local area coverage? Is there enough use to pay for the added system centers? Are the savings large enough to pay for the usable options? We need to capture, weigh, and test these results and trade-offs in the changing world of market coverage and shared usage.

The Customers

Most marketplace events cover a wide range of using groups and customers. Branch banks deal with many types of customers: retail customers, branches of small companies, corporate branches, trust customers, and others. In a branch bank, with many manual tasks, most customers are forced into the same mold. They are served in a like manner through a limited number of branch staffs and staff types. If we use communications-based banking units and systems, this mold can be broken, or at least might confine us less. We now enjoy a chance to tailor service to each customer type. Therefore, in preparing a plan you will find it worthwhile to look for those service needs that are unique to each type of major user. Document those service needs. Seek the marketplace events that use these services. Consider new self-service or remote service usage based on unique needs.

Office or Working Area Space

Space needs may be a valuable subject for a planning study. New space additions during the planning period may create new sources of activity. As the new space becomes usable and active, we must consider it for future demands. Also, we must examine future plans for new space demands. For example, use of paper checks is expected to fall to zero growth in the next few years. However, between now and zero growth, the volume of paper checks will increase. Where will we process these added checks in the meanwhile? Will we have enough space for the equipment and people to provide the added check processing service? In any event, we should consider that space may be a key subject for study and planning.

Current Activities

Some plans do not cover the current or old activities. The growth in the use of paper checks, just mentioned, may be one of these. Such areas need to be reviewed, future changes estimated, and key values documented for review in future planning cycles. Space can be costly. The lead time it requires create costly delays. An early view of these "old" activity needs can save or avoid some last-minute problems in planning.

Other Market Factors

Other marketplace forces can affect your future. A new government requirement for reporting is one example. A new tax law, such as the law that created the new IRA accounts, may require action in the marketplace. More likely, a move by your competition can cause marketplace changes.

A set of future marketplace events must consider the likelihood of events from these causes. In banking, reduced interstate limitations, changing paper check usage, or a new fee schedule may be likely action plan events. For each possible event you need estimates of response and impact. Also, the resources needed to respond to these moves must be estimated and shown in the plan.

THE ROLE OF THE USERS

Test the Results

The users must be prime judges of the plan results. They must live with the results of the planning process. Therefore, the users must know at an early point whether the plan will give the results they expect and need. Will the plan produce the needed marketplace events? Will the events produce the needed results for staff and output? To answer these questions requires that tests be applied to the action plans and key values. Several of these tests are as follows:

- Are the marketplace events and goals of highest priority?
- Does the events' content, sequence, and timing match the users' needs?
- Are the key values correct for the required results?
- Are the staff output and key event results as shown?
- Are the projections of results real?
- Are the correct key values documented?
- Does the staff, space, and output growth compare with plan goals?
- Does usage per work station provide for a reasonable load on each?
- Are there enough work station users to provide the planned usage?
- Are there enough events to account for the output changes over the plan period?
- Can you attract the necessary customer and account growth to meet the plan needs?

- Can you install the work stations within the period specified?
- Can you support the marketplace events with marketing and staff action plans?
- Is the projected market growth realizable?
- Are the costs and income flow in the plan realizable?
- Are some customers not worth having in the plan?

You need to answer these and like questions now. Now is the time to thrash out the marketplace events and their results. A joint review of these and like questions by user and data processing personnel will avoid later drastic changes in the plan steps that follow.

Move with Joint User and Data Processing Plans

Both users and data processing personnel have helped create the joint plan. Both groups are necessary to achieve the action plans. Now is the time for the users to make their views heard. If the users agree with the plan, then they must put their own support plans in place. These user support plans include the following examples:

- Marketing
- Staff education
- Plastic card marketing
- Customer education
- New branch locations
- Advertising
- Media preparation (such as card design)
- Self-service banking site selection

Only joint action plans by the processing staff and users will provide results that match and support the plan's content and timetable.

Get Top Management Support

At this point you will have produced and tested a market plan. You have shown the users how it will help them, and they support the approach. A set of content tests have been applied successfully. You stated the plans and goals in terms of key values. The plan elements have set the sequence and timing of future events. Now you need the support of top management. This approval step precedes the system resource study step. But this step will be repeated after the system resources have been assessed.

By getting management support now, you are less likely to face drastic changes later. Top-level support also sets the stage so that the next plan steps happen when they should. You will have many points in the next steps at which you can revise or fine-tune the plan goals, test expenses, and review timetables.

○
○
○
Step 3:
○
Anticipating System
○
○
and Development
○
Resources
○

CHAPTER GOALS

Convert future marketplace events into system resource needs.

Convert transactions to messages.

Convert message arrivals into processing loads.

Convert application and customer record needs to data base storage.

Document the conversion process and results.

INTRODUCTION

Converting numerically quantified marketplace events into system resources is a well-known estimating technique in data processing. The topic is presented here to demonstrate the process to the participants in the planning process who are not familiar with data processing. It is presented to show the ease of this step in the plan. This step is vital if the planning process is to show an early view of resource needs for the data processing system. That early view is needed in order to develop system capacity on a timely basis. Timely actions help to avoid or minimize constraints on marketplace action.

PRINCIPLES IN THE EXAMPLE (REFER TO CHAPTER 2)

Projection of Market Events

Marketplace events may be numerically quantified. The events can be described in terms of the number of customers, accounts, facilities, branches, staffs, and other key factors. These numeric values may be estimated for future events. This process was demonstrated in the example. Also, it was shown in the description of step 2: projecting marketplace events. These numeric values are basic to making a realistic long-range plan. They are needed for resource measuring. The numeric values are also used to test the marketplace results versus business goals.

The transactions that result from marketplace events may be related to both customers and to the applications being performed. They may be used to calculate the staffs needed to provide the services and the planned improvements. The growth in transaction volumes may be related to the growth of the marketplace activities. These numeric results may be shown in terms of their effect on the key results. For example, consider the planned improvements in teller output: these may be used to slow staff growth. The growth change may be shown in a count of staff growth avoided. Also, its impact may be shown by skill type. This process is the basis for estimating system resource growth. This process helps to make a successful long-range plan, that is, one whose results may be projected and compared with their related objectives.

Work Stations

Future marketplace events require individual activities. These may be used by staff members, employees in user departments, or customers operating self-service devices. For each of these activities, an interface with the data processing system is provided by some type of work station. The number of work stations required may be derived from the size of the user group. However, the total number should reflect the actual installation rates. As shown in the example, it may take several years to complete the installation of the projected number of work stations. The plan results will show the build-up rate of work stations as well as the total number expected. The number of work stations is used to size several parts of the system resources, such as converting work stations counts to terminal units. Terminals, which include keyboards, displays, printers, and similar units, are the actual input and output units that interface with the data processing system. The number of work stations also contributes to fixing the network message load.

Assessing the Economics

A quick economic assessment was provided in the example. It first found the avoided or delayed expense growth in space and staff. It then compared the needs avoided with the increased expense of the added work stations. It also included the expense of the intallation and system attachment needed to achieve the improvement plans. These quantified events will also become an input to the process of quantifying the system resources. It is important that these input values be pretested and confirmed. This testing confirms that the quantities give the right results and helps to avoid unnecessary repetition of the system resource quantification. Still more important, it helps to avoid use of untested entry data. Untested input data may provide an incorrect quantifying of the required system resources. Several suggested tests of the values for marketplace quantifying were described in step 2.

CONVERTING TRANSACTIONS TO MESSAGES

What Is a Transaction?

Each transaction has a purpose, which must be understood in order to design an adequate data processing system. Transactions are handled through a work station connected to the system. Each transaction creates a series of messages. A message is the movement of a group of data items between work station and the system; it may concern authorizing, controlling, or locating data in the system. Messages are the communications building blocks of each transaction. Messages structure a sequence of movements of the data needed to respond to and complete the transaction at the work station.

Example of a Message

Consider an automatic teller machine transaction: The ATM is started by a customer inserting a magnetic plastic card, then entering a personal identification number (PIN), selecting a transaction request (such as withdrawing cash), and entering a transaction amount. The automatic teller machine prepares and sends a message through the network to an authorizing or control point, which is the system control point with access to the customer's account balance data.

The *first* message is a request for authorization to dispense. Generally, this message includes the following types of data:

- Identification of the customer
- Customer's personal identification number (PIN)
- Amount of cash requested
- Account source of the funds (savings or checking account)
- Identification of the automatic teller machine
- Some or all of the data recorded on the magnetic-striped plastic card
- Random or nonrepetitive number to make this message unique

Selected portions of the message data are encrypted (coded) for protection of vital message data.

Customer identification includes identification of the financial institution that issued the card. That specific institution is responsible for transactions entered into by the card holder. Using the issuer identification, the data processing network can route the message to the issuer system or to a designated authorization point. Upon receipt of the message at the authorization point an "application" program takes appropriate steps, including steps to evaluate and respond to the request. The selectively encrypted portions (random digits) are checked to assure that the message is a legitimate request. The related or customer data is retrieved and examined to see if the customer has enough funds to respond to the request. The card number is also checked against current "hot" lists of lost and stolen cards. The account number is checked against activity lists to assure that the card usage has not exceeded current activity limits, which include the total amount of dollars issued and the number of times the card was used in a given period. These steps provide tests for stolen cards and other abnormal situations.

Upon completion of the application program steps, a response message is created and transmitted to the sending point, the ATM. The response message is designed to tell the ATM what actions it may now take. The ATM may issue cash; it may refuse the transaction by returning the card and directing the customer to a branch staff member; or it may refuse the transaction and retain the card to prevent further abuse of the account by unauthorized card usage. Not all ATMs are instructed to retain cards or have a retention capability.

The *second* or response message to the originating ATM generally contains the following types of data:

- ○ Identification of the automatic teller machine
- ○ Identification of the customer
- ○ Amount of funds that may be dispensed
- ○ A random or nonrepetitive number to make the message unique

Selected portions of the message are encrypted for communications protection of vital message data.

Finishing the Transaction

Upon receipt of the second or response message, the automatic teller machine checks that the message is valid, then completes the transaction with the customer. Currency is counted and dispensed; a transaction record is printed; and both cash and record slip are presented to the customer. The initiating card is available for the customer.

As part of the completion process a *third* message is prepared and sent by the ATM. This message advises the control or application point that the transaction has been successfully completed. Several conditions, such as a power failure, might arise after the authorization or response message, resulting in an incomplete or partial action. Therefore, the final results need to be communicated for a complete activity record.

The *third* or completion message generally contains the following data:

○ Identification of the customer

○ Identification of the automatic teller machine

○ Amount of funds dispensed

○ Confirmation of transaction completion or a code to show the actual result

The third message completes the account record updating. It is used for the activity journal entries and other appropriate system records and controls.

As a result of this sequence of three messages, the conversion factor for transactions to messages for automatic teller machines transactions is 1:3, or 1 transaction to 3 messages. In each transaction case the actual conversion factor is fixed by a combination of work station design and the application program interface. Within your data processing management group, this conversion factor is a design choice. This group has the know-how to state the factors to be used for conversion of transaction types to network message counts. It is possible for the factor to be less than one, such as 1.0:0.2 or 5 transactions to 1 message. This indicates that several transactions are combined into a single message. This might occur in an activity of the data capture type. In some instances, part of the message stream may be combined: in the case of an automatic teller machine, two or more successive transactions might be combined, resulting in a ratio of 1.0:2.5 or 1 ATM transaction per 2½ messages.

Message Documentation

For each application area, the transaction types and volumes are recorded, message conversion rate is added, and the total message volume captured. The volumes are generally the average counts over a given period. However, identification of the peak period and the ratio of peak to average message volumes is also recorded. The transaction volumes must be limited to the actual build-up rates and total numbers for work stations installation. This process limits the transaction volumes to those that may be entered through installed units only. This also distributes the message volume build-up over several years, based on transaction growth forecasts and installation rates for work stations.

Message Volume Growth

Generally transaction volumes and their messages grow in proportion to customer acceptance and usage. The results grow in proportion to the underlying applications or new services. Growth in the number of plastic card owners increases the number of card users who are active. However, there must be available a reasonable quantity of machines in which to use the cards. Thus growth in active cards increases the card-based services proportionately. This growth occurs only if the cards and the related services are in the same geographic area. In some applications there may be a lesser ceiling on the activity, as when only a lower percentage of accounts accept cards and use the cards actively. These lower limits should be used to constrain the maximum transaction and message volumes accordingly. In other words, plan on realistically achievable activity volumes—not theoretical maximums.

Documentation Tables

The table for transactions and their messages should record the appropriate values for each major application area. Documentation examples are shown in detail in the Report Outline (appendix 2), which contains an outline of plan content. An assumption table, with entry examples, might appear as shown in table 5-1.

The transaction: message ratio values are applied to the transaction volumes. The resulting message volumes should be calculated and documented as shown in table 5-2.

Additional documentation should be provided when the following factors are not easily determined from the foregoing tables:

- ○ Average transaction and message volumes per second
- ○ Period identification for average and peak volumes
- ○ Ratio of peak to average volumes per second

Other important message characteristics include geographic distribution of message activity, which is needed when transaction activity is not distributed according to the normal customer/account distribution.

Future Network Traffic

An important consideration in estimating future network capacity requirements is to determine how many networks are involved and which messages are carried on which network. Many organizations have multiple networks: those for data, voice, security, environmental control, facsimile, electronic message or mail, word processing, video or videotex, and several other types. It is economically desirable to concentrate the traffic from several networks into one, thereby reducing line costs and achieving an economy of scale. Combining the traffic into one network may permit the use of larger capacity links with a lower cost per message; for example, you might be able to use a

Table 5-1

APPLICATION AREA	TRANSACTION TYPE	TRANSACTION: MESSAGE RATIO	SOURCE OF ASSUMPTION	LEVEL OF CONFIDENCE
1	1	$N_1:N_2$	Department,	High,
2	2	$N_3:N_4$	person,	medium,
3	3	$N_5:N_6$	test	low

Table 5-2

	AVERAGE MONTHLY MESSAGE VOLUMES BY YEAR						
	-3	-2	-1	1	2	3	N
Average monthly message volume per transaction type							
Type 1							
Type 2							
Type N							
Total monthly message volume							
% annual growth in monthly message volumes							
% overall growth in monthly message volumes since year -1							

satellite link between two cities that have a dense traffic pattern.

Unfortunately, at this time, care must be taken in combining networks. Do not assume too quickly that all types of communications can be directly mixed in a single network. Voice-type traffic has characteristics different from data that has been digitalized for transmission. Voice signals may be mixed over the same network facilities. However, it takes appropriate equipment and network routing. Current network design may have limitations that impair the performance of combined voice and digital data networks. Make sure that any network decision beyond those of the digital data projections includes experts from your network management department. In fact, that management should be coordinating this vital projection of system resources.

Network Planning

Objectives of the long-range planning process regarding networks are as follows:

○ Achieve combined network use to maximize network economics.

○ Optimize the network economics through the use of high-density links where practical and available. Use improved economic solutions such as a satellite link. Consider such solutions where the projections of future loads show an adequate routing need and economic return.

○ Use projections of future network growth to adjust the system design. Also, increase the installed capacity at an early point in time, early enough to order adequate capacity on a continuing basis. This avoids undue delays or periods of inadequate capacity.

○ Designate a computer network management responsibility. Direct it to provide adequate network capacity, design choices, operation, and performance. (This subject is covered further in step 4: reviewing implementation support.)

CONVERTING MESSAGES
TO PROCESSING LOAD PROJECTIONS

Messages are designed to interact with application processing programs. The application program directs the process that recognizes and responds to a message request. The application program arranges for access to the appropriate data base records and applies the logic necessary to prepare a response to the message. It updates the related records, journals, and output areas, and completes the transaction processing. In an "on-line, interactive" system the messages tend to initiate the routine processing activities. In a "batch" type of system usage, an ordered set of entry data records are brought to the processor. Each output data record is then used to initiate the updating of the related data base records.

In either case the data processing requirements are projectable. These time needs are from either measurements of current actual processor run lengths or assumptions of conventional processor load timing. These timing assumptions relate to processing complexity. They are extended by message arrival rates or counts of entry records. In addition, processing time computation techniques provide estimates for the growth in processing times. The growth relates to increases in those factors that describe job growth, such as the number of customers and transactions. Changes may also result from an increase in arrival rates, growing processing complexity, increased batch sizes, or similar changes. The projected growth factors provide an estimate of the total processing capacity growth needs. These needs are expressed in instruction executions per unit of time—usually a second. Your data processing system capacity and performance staff can provide an appropriate set of estimating factors.

Projecting Processing Loads

The process by which processing loads may be projected is as follows:

○ Identify major processing use by application area and operating mode (on-line or batch).

○ Project the expected growth in terms of messages, input record volumes, or transaction growth for each major application area.

○ Relate the process time needed to input volumes.

○ Extend the processing time required in proportion to the relationships established between input growth and processing time needed.

○ Establish a set of planning factors for other processing time usage: these should include program and system development and testing. Also, include backup and configuration contingency needs. Processing loads for development of new applications and fallback capacity for the on-line system are also to be estimated.

New applications processing times may be estimated by using assumptions of complexity and input volume in comparison with known processing jobs.

Processing time should be allocated for an information center operation. This is a self-service application development facility for the using departments to develop their own programs. These efforts are for short, one-time, or experimental efforts. These tasks do not generally justify the use of a dedicated application development facility today. (More on this subject in step 4.)

Processing units come in fixed increments of performance capacity. Generally the next largest processing unit is ordered when the total processing load is determined. There may also be a configuration issue: that is, a processor dedicated to the support of an on-line network needs to be replaced by another dedicated processor in case of emergency. These considerations tend to result in an additional processing capacity gap because of imperfect loading of the available units. This situation may be further exaggerated when equipment is ordered to accommodate peakloads. The net result is a "geometry" problem of determining total capacity needs and the number and size of the units that best fit the needs.

Processing Load Documentation

Appendix 2 covers a complete management report, including a set of planning documentation. The suggested documentation for this area covers the assumptions made and the added capacity considerations listed previously. The assumptions may be documented as in table 5-3.

NOTE: These assumptions should be documented for each major application area. When actual experience of processing run time is unavailable, an expert estimate should be used. The results of subsequent development experience may then be used to update these estimates. This is done in later cycles of the planning process.

The assumptions of the processing load include an identified relationship to a measurement of input or transaction volume. This volume measurement was forecast in tables 5-1 and 5-2. By using the expected volume growth and its assumed relation to processing load, a total processing load may be estimated for the planning period. A suggested format for this documentation is shown in table 5-4.

Processing Load Charting

In using the results of estimates of the processing load it is necessary to determine the proper point at which to order additional capacity. One interesting way to visualize these relationships is to use the technique shown in table 5-5 for processing load capacity charting.

The "processing capacity" increments represent the capacity of currently available processing units. The processing load is expressed in MIPS (millions of instruction executions per second). The processing load may be converted to future increments in processing capacity as future computer capacity in MIPS is determined. In subsequent planning iterations, the processing loads and capacity projections may be updated to reflect the later machine capacities and capacity needs. The processing capacity update in later plan cycles also provides an opportunity to quantify the changes and to identify the reasons for change.

PROJECTING DEVELOPMENT NEEDS

The application load described in the processor load computations requires a forecast of the load for application program

Table 5-3

APPLICATION AREA	MODE TYPE*	PROCESSING COMPLEXITY	TRANSACTION VOLUMES	SOURCE OF ASSUMPTION; CONFIDENCE LEVEL
1	On-line, batch, in-line, real-time, batch in specified time period, etc.	High, medium, low	Quantity	Department; high, medium or low
2				
3				
N				

*On-line: post at time of transaction, but time may expand to given limit. In-line: post as soon after transaction as possible. Real-time: post within specified time interval.

Table 5–4

	PROCESSING CAPACITY BY YEAR (MIPS)*						
	-3	-2	-1	1	2	3	N
Application area							
1							
2							
3							
N							
Total application processing							
Other needs							
New application development							
Information center use							
Development/testing							
Etc.							
Total active processing							
Backup/Contingency							
Imperfect loading							
Total processing							
% annual growth in processing capacity							
% overall growth in processing capacity since year -1							

*MIPS = millions of instruction executions per second.

Table 5–5

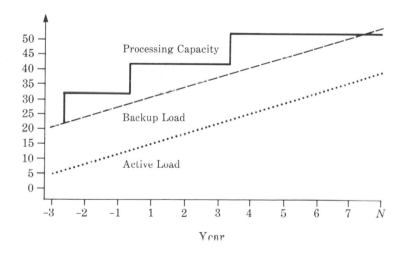

development. As these forecasts are prepared, they may be documented as in the following tables. Preparation of development work load estimates is a well-known technique. The key challenge is to compare the composite work loads for new and for existing activities. The pressing need is to free resources from existing maintenance activities. Once freed, these resources may be applied to the new project area. Table 5–6 shows how well this transition is taking place in your organization.

The program development resource is projected in person-months of effort. This is estimated from several factors that are well known in the development planning area. Note the line item for other needs: maintenance. This is especially important, since up to 75 percent of total resources may be devoted to this category. If so, then it may be desirable to show the category broken into its major components.

Generally programmer productivity is measured in output per unit of person effort, measures that are well known in program estimating activities. The objective in table 5–7 is to show the continued improvement in the output of personnel in the

Table 5–6

	DEVELOPMENT WORK LOAD BY YEAR (PERSON-MONTHS)*						
	-3	-2	-1	1	2	3	N
Development area							
New project 1							
New project 2							
New project 3							
New project N							
Total new projects							
Other staff needs							
Maintenance							
Education							
New techniques							
Etc.							
Total of all staff needs							
% annual growth in work load							
% overall growth in work load since year -1							

* Person-months = number of persons assigned × number of months of effort.

Table 5-7

	PROGRAM DEVELOPMENT PRODUCTIVITY BY YEAR (PERSON-MONTHS)						
	-3	-2	-1	1	2	3	N
Development area							
New projects							
Old projects							
Total output							
% annual growth in program development productivity							
% overall growth in program development productivity since year -1							

development activities. This is usually measured in "programming units" (e.g., lines of code) per person-month. The important goal is to force an improvement. One method is to force these activities out of the development house. Getting users to do their own application development is one technique. Another is to use packages that have been developed by outside groups. The remaining resource should show continued improvement through the use of improved techniques and better management approaches.

CONVERTING APPLICATIONS TO DATA STORAGE NEEDS

Data storage is used in several ways in a data processing system. The message processing program initiates the commands to obtain the data base records. The program processes the entry data, updates it, and then returns the records to the data storage devices in accordance with the application and system needs. The quantity of data base records required is generally in proportion to the number of customer account records required. Other uses of data storage include working storage areas for input messages and data records, intermediate results storage, and output results storage. Another storage use is for the multiple generations of master files needed for security and recovery needs. These areas are needed in case of equipment breakdown or the loss of the main customer or account records. As with estimates of processing loads, there is also a need to support other activities, such as development, testing, new application growth, information center use, and backup. The approach to estimating data storage requirements is quite similar to the processing capacity technique discussed previously. Your data processing system capacity and performance group can provide the appropriate estimating factors.

Projecting Data Storage Needs

Data storage is called on as required to respond to the instructions in the application program. Obtaining, for example, a customer record may require several accesses into a direct-access storage device: first, an access to determine the address of the customer record; then an access to get the customer record; followed by an access to return the updated record to the storage area. There are probably several more accesses for audit journals, working totals, and output preparation. The time required for these data base access activities has been provided for in the total time for the processing programs. The need at this point is to quantify the amount of data storage needed for these application support functions. The process by which data storage needs are projected is as follows:

- Identify the major data base or data storage needs for each application area and operating mode: take the number of account records and extend it by the estimated storage needs for each application area.

- Project the expected growth of accounts or transactions (or both) for each application area.

- Extend the data storage required in proportion to the relation established between growth in data storage and growth in account records or transactions (or both).

- Establish a set of planning factors for other data storage usage. Include development and testing, information center use, new applications, multiple master files for backup and security, intermediate working storage, and input/output needs.

New application storage requirements can be estimated with record count and content projections. This is done by comparison with experience in known data storage.

As with processing capacity, data storage capacity comes in reasonably large increments of size and a wide range of performance characteristics. However, the selection and fitting process is beyond the scope of this planning process. These techniques are well-known by your capacity and performance planning staff. (More on the system capacity and performance function in step 4.)

Data Storage Documentation

Documentation is necessary for the capacity needs of the on-line direct access storage device. This documentation covers the key relationships between customer record and transaction growth and data base growth. A suggested format is shown in table 5-8.

These assumptions should be documented for each major area of data base. When actual data base capacity needs are not available, an expert guess may be used. The results of later development or pilot activities may be used to update these estimates in later planning cycles. This, in turn, updates the assumptions and resource quantifications. The direct access storage device capacity needs are usually expressed in hundreds of millions of characters or bytes (100 MBs).

A suggested data storage capacity projection documentation format is shown in table 5-9.

Table 5-8

APPLICATION AREA	ACCOUNT RECORDS	TRANSACTION VOLUME PER ACCOUNT RECORD	SOURCE OF ASSUMPTION; CONFIDENCE LEVEL
1	Volume	Ratio	Department,
2			high, medium,
3			low
N			

Table 5–9

	DATA STORAGE NEEDS BY YEAR (100 MEGABYTES)						
	-3	-2	-1	1	2	3	N
Application area							
1							
2							
3							
N							
Total application storage							
Other needs							
New application development							
Information center use							
Development/testing							
Working storage							
Master file copies							
Total active storage							
Backup/Contingency							
Imperfect loading							
Total storage							
% annual growth in data storage needs							
% overall growth in data storage needs since year -1							

PRACTICAL CONSIDERATIONS

Estimating system resource is, as we said at the beginning of this step, a well-practiced technique. It is accomplished to various degrees of refinement depending upon the available entry data and a management's expressed need. In this planning process, the major emphasis has been on specifying and quantifying future marketplace events. The quantification has been related to key input factors. Once completed, these quantified dimensions have become the system resource estimating base. You'll have no great difficulty in completing this phase after the initial event identification and quantification. The factors will be found between data processing system management and your vendors' expertise. Hence, the description of this step is designed only to familiarize you with the entire planning process. It is quite appropriate to rely on your data processing system planning experts for specifics, but on your terms: that is, the priority need is for these experts to accept, support, and implement the marketplace event projections. Only when quantified and timed with their support will you get timely accomplishment.

○
○
Step 4: Reviewing
○
Implementation Support
○

CHAPTER GOALS

Determine the implementation support activities needed.

Inventory the implementation support needed.

Assess the implementation support organization.

Assess the readiness of implementation activities to achieve the needed plan.

THE IMPLEMENTATION SUPPORT CHALLENGE

Need for Implementation Support

The evolution of future data processing systems will be marked by major challenges. There will be a greater use of communications and network facilities. This means shifting to an on-line, data base oriented, interactive mode of application processing. Electronics will replace paper with direct access and interaction to data storage and with direct responses to the entering work stations. The work stations will be directly operated by staff, by user department employees, and by customers at self-service units.

An added characteristic of these future systems will be the need for a smooth transition in system design and implementation from the batch mode to the on-line mode of operation. This change will require the data processing staffs to obtain new skills and responsibilities. Managing change will require new management concepts and capabilities with the efficient processes that are needed to initiate, design, develop, test, implement, and track these new data processing capabilities. The process will require new high-productivity techniques of application and system programming in order to allow a finite number of skilled people to cope with the growing workload of new projects. All-in-all, new operating goals will be the way of life for the data processing organization.

The Purpose of Step 4

The purpose of the step is to prepare you—the nontechnical manager associated with this long-range plan process—with these new capabilities for system and application implementation; also, to explain to you the role of the new capabilities in making future marketplace events occur on a timely and successful basis with full data processing support. Hence, there is a need to make you fully aware of the major areas of data processing system implementation.

The long-range planning process needs to establish the status of the major implementation activities. Then the process needs to direct these activities toward achieving the marketplace events within a planned budget and resource allowance. One way to assure a successful implementation process is to put in place a continuous process of reviewing the functional work content and status of the implementation at regular intervals. The review can check on assignments and the results of implementation support activities.

The major challenge to you is to contain the size, expand the use, and assure the responsiveness of these resources. You will be pleasantly surprised at your ability, as a nonexpert in processing, to assess these issues and their status. However, you must get beyond the fog-bound coast of nomenclature and responsibilities. As the responsible planning process manager, you need to assure that the plans for data processing implementation will directly assist the users in achieving their projected marketplace events.

What You Learn from Step 4

It is not the purpose of this step to give you an in-depth technical education. Nor will this step give you the details necessary for the day-to-day technical management of the functions being reviewed. You will learn a good deal in the review process; however, it takes skilled professionals to implement data processing correctly and on time. You will, therefore, be involved in the hiring, directing, evaluating, and managing of the technical personnel that manage and staff these implementation support activities. The degree to which you succeed in achieving your marketplace events on a timely basis depends on your skill in managing these activities. You need to understand the data processing staff's operations sufficiently to set goals, to measure results, and confirm progress, as well as to supervise budgets, schedules, plan content, and staffing actions. All of these responsibilities require a better appreciation of the implementation support roles and activities and how they directly relate to achieving the long-range plan.

There is no substitute for effective, well-trained management of these implementation support activities. However, nontechnical managers, without prior data processing experience, have successfully coped with these issues at the management and planning level. What is required is a nontechnical understanding of the content and intent of these responsibilities. The approach to be followed here helps you play a more effective planning and status evaluation role.

The Implementation Support Assessment Approach

The basic approach to this area consists of a nontechnical description of the purpose of each implementation area. This means you need to understand the activities provided in a nontechnical way. You need to compare each activity with the implementation support demands to be satisfied, in order to make the future plans and events occur successfully. These implementation demands include the management, design, development, and operational issues. There are additional discoveries you are seeking as you examine each of the implementation components of an area plan, such as staffing, budget, and work load: Are there any hidden constraints? What action options are available? How will those actions speed your efforts while using your resources more productively?

The Basic Questions

In a review of each of the implementation activities, the following nontechnical questions will be used to obtain a status and direction assessment. You must rely on the management of each area to assist you and to respond to you by providing answers. It is preferable that the answers be documented in a succinct and simple manner for a later review. (See appendix 2 for a documentation outline.) Documentation provides a base for a consistent evaluation between successive planning cycles.

The basic issues to be examined for each implementation area are as follows:

ORGANIZATIONAL RESPONSIBILITY

○ What are the organizational responsibilities for each implementation activity?

○ Who are the responsible first-line and second-line managers?

- To whom does the staff of this activity report?
- How is the activity identified within the organization or in the allocation of functional responsibilities?

CURRENT OBJECTIVES

- What are the current objectives of the activity?
- How are the objectives quantitatively described and measured?
- How does the staff of this activity know if it is successful in achieving its objectives?
- How is success defined?

FUTURE WORKLOAD

- What is the future workload for each activity?
- How is the workload measured?
- What is the process for starting, tracking, and stopping projects?
- How has the future workload been projected or assigned?
- How is the workload numerically measured?
- How is the activity evaluated for performance?

ACTIVITY TIMETABLES

- What is the timetable for completion of future activities?
- How are the timetables set?
- Are there any planned intermediate checkpoints?
- How does the staff of this activity know if the time targets will be satisfied?
- To whom is the time progress reported and how?

ASSIGNED RESOURCES

○ What is the assigned budget, including funds and head-count?

○ In which organizational department is the budget reflected?

○ What has been the budget growth characteristics for the last 3 years? Why?

○ What is the future budget projection for at least 4 years? Why?

○ Where does the personnel come from?

○ Is the personnel permanently assigned or is it borrowed for tasks?

○ Are the funds assigned or allocated by project or plan objective?

○ If allocated by management, how are the allocations and priorities established?

DOCUMENTATION AND REPORTS

○ How is the activity documented and reported?

○ How are the projects described?

○ How is progress tracked and recorded?

○ How and when are the results reviewed and reported to management?

MANAGEMENT CONTROLS

○ When and how often are reviews made?

○ How are they made?

○ Who participates?

○ How are these activities coordinated with those of other groups

- Are there joint plan reviews and status reports?
- What roles are played by top management, the user departments, and the data processing top management in tracking progress versus planning?
- Are there new project proposals?
- Who participates with which decisions on whether to proceed with new proposals?
- Are there projections of required resources, system performance, and capacity?
- Are the earlier projections for capacity, performance, and resource reassessed at implementation time?
- Are prior estimates tracked at the checkpoints?
- Is the estimation process and assumptions documented and tracked to improve future estimates?

SUCCESS MEASUREMENTS

- What are the success measures?
- Are available options understood and exercised?
- What are the quantitative success factors?
- Have unsuccessful efforts been redirected? And with what quantitative considerations and results?
- How are options to decommit, to change timetables, and to add resources reviewed with the other participants?
- What is the activity measurement output per unit of budget or resource?
- How has it changed and how is it projected to change over time?

These latter factors are of particular importance in application and system development activities.

THE MAJOR IMPLEMENTATION
SUPPORT AREAS

There are four areas of implementation support activities, which represent a logical combination of goals and effort. They are presented as guides, and you may wish to rearrange them to adjust to the realities of your environment. The implementation support groups are as follows:

MANAGEMENT AND PLANNING RESPONSIBILITIES

The management process is for new data processing projects. It spans the project preparation process from proposal to postcompletion review. This process also supports a continuous planning process and makes use of these planning process results between planning cycles.

DESIGN AND EVOLUTION RESPONSIBILITIES

These are the primary technical staff activities that guide and direct your data processing organization and system as it evolves. These activities mold the data processing system in order to achieve the results visualized in the long-range plan.

OPERATION AND CONTROL ACTIVITIES

This covers the day-to-day activities that manage your data processing system. These activities are used to state and achieve the data processing performance and availability goals. Availability is defined as determining whether the equipment is running when it is wanted for use. Availability is essential if the system is to be successful and competitive in the world of on-line, interactive systems.

DEVELOPMENT MANAGEMENT RESPONSIBILITIES

This activity comprises the supervision, the skills, and the project efforts required to turn plan content into operative application and system programs. This must be done while achieving increased productivity in using development resources. Success is the achievement of productive results on a timely and cost-effective basis.

The Significance of These Implementation Activities

These activities are really the life-cycle steps in a rapidly evolving and modernizing data processing organization and system. These issues and events span the spectrum from recognizing marketplace needs and formulating solutions through assessing implementations to confirming results. To some, this assessment of implementation support may be out of place in a planning process. However, to avoid consideration of these issues here would be to separate "What to do?" from "Can we get it done?" To be realistic, these issues must be considered together. They offer each other numerous opportunities for trade-offs and action alternatives as resources are balanced against desires. Consideration of the alternatives is necessary, even imperative, if you are to achieve the desired end results. You have a broad range of time, budget, and staffing options. However, you must know and take advantage of these options if you are to succeed within a reasonable expense of resources.

The Documentation Format

To outline this array of implementation issues—in a nontechnical manner—a simple documentation format is provided for each. Included are the task assigned, the relation to the overall process, and a description of a criteria for success.

Note that many of these staff activities do not involve large functional groups. Rather, they are small but technically talented skill groups. Do not confuse the amount of responsibility with the number of persons assigned. In most cases a small investment in a needed support activity returns the investment many times over in efficiency, economies, and achievements.

Let us consider each implementation support activity in more detail.

MANAGEMENT AND PLANNING RESPONSIBILITIES

This activity maintains a continuous planning process in which both the data processing users and data processing providing department actively and cooperatively contribute. The objective is to formalize the planning process with a few selected top-level executives. This is an added responsibility assigned to these few key planning executives. This top management acts as a planning process supervision and review committee. The planning process executives assure that the plan and its documentation are maintained on a continuous basis. They achieve the communication of content, changes, and updated material to all designated receivers. They prepare for the next iteration of the planning process. They provide interim studies when required by changing circumstances. They prepare statistical and quantitative data for each planning cycle starting point. Planning is on an 18-month to 24-month cycle at most. The later cycles are used to confirm the major trends, report status, and propose event changes. The planning process executives report to top management on a periodic basis with changes to the plan and the planning process. Reporting on a quarterly basis is probably appropriate.

Interim Studies

Between planning cycles there will be interim studies that focus on areas of quick change or major decision needs. The studies may be in depth. The study results need to be carried foward in a documented form for inclusion in the next planning process cycle. The plan supervision committee also supervises the new project review process (to be described next). This process controls plan changes between plan cycles.

As interim efforts are completed, the results will be selectively distributed and reported to top management. Computer techniques exist and may be used to mechanize a major part of the planning process, documentation, and distribution. Techniques to quickly provide mathematical models of the computational processes of the system resources and capture numeric value relations and measures should be used. These techniques will also allow a quicker and more thorough examination of alternatives between planning cycles.

A New Project Management Process

This activity offers a phased evolutionary process that allows effective management of all major data processing development projects. The phases cover the life span from proposal to a post-implementation assessment. The phases include proposal, design, development, testing and implementation, and postimplementation assessment. The start of each phase is made by setting an objective, by providing estimates of development and system resource use, and making a projection of the implementation support impact. Each phase is concluded with a phase completion assessment, which is a validation of the entry estimates and a reaffirmation of the impact projection. Successful phase completion allows initiation of the next phase. The phase review participants include all interested parties—users, implementation support staff, and data processing providing department management.

An important part of each phase is the users' participation. They play an important role in providing the impact value of marketplace events. The value of this phased evolutionary process, during the early phases, is to alert all participants. The estimates prepare each group for their role in the successful completion of a project. This includes a timely ordering of system capacity and the scheduling of development resource assignments. Also, the phased evolutionary process commits staff participation and confirms budget estimates. Phase content and status documentation is an excellent adjunct to the continuous planning cycle process. Success of this phased evolutionary activity is determined by the participation of key management and the progress of successful phase completions. These factors help to ensure that planned marketplace events with data processing support occur on a timely and economic basis.

DESIGN AND EVOLUTION RESPONSIBILITIES

General Role

These activities, which fall within the data processing providing department's responsibilities, are like the architecture and design of a house, but a design that is changed with each new marketplace event. Does the house keep the occupants happy as it evolves? Is the house building budget keeping within control? Are the changes taking place on schedule? If so, then the architects are on the right track. When required parts of the house are not recognized or designed on time, are unavailable, or are unsuitable, then the architects have fallen down on the job.

The staff assigned this responsibility participates in the phase review process in order to detect any area of required change. Early sensitivity to potential problems assures success later—when it counts—in actual implementation and marketplace results.

System Architecture Responsibility

This staff responsibility develops the system configuration, the modes of operation, and the system evolution plan. Under what rules are the system components selected, integrated, and organized? Several issues are supervised by this group. Included is software (programming systems) selection for operation and for data base and data communications design alternatives, and system evaluation, transition plans, and new operating requirements. Architecture rules must provide for high availability. Distributed system use and operation are among some of the other results expected. Success of this staff responsibility is measured by its ability to evolve the system on a timely basis. The system must accommodate the new support required for successful achievement of the marketplace event plans. Architectural plans must be set sufficiently early to allow completion of development and implementation activities as they are required.

Network Architecture and Design

The objective of this activity is to provide the communications network capacity plan and design to support future evolution of the data processing system, and to support the achievement of the required marketplace events. Some of the lead times in this area are challenging, especially when the required lines and communications facilities have long order times. Sometimes lines are unavailable or have high and escalating charges. Occasionally communication facilities are subject to rapidly changing regulatory rules and offerings.

This activity projects the network capacity and users' requirements. It works closely with the communications network management department that uses the projections to order capacity, installs equipment, and designs the network routings. This department knows the communications options and economics that are available. It tracks new facility concepts to match existing or projected needs. Development is aided to achieve the best economics and service plan within time and budget constraints. It supervises the network and data transmission security. The security rules are set by determining where the security risks and exposures exist and which are the appropriate lines of defense. Success is judged by the end results. Good results are a plan with adequate and timely capacity to support the planned marketplace events.

Capacity and Performance Assurance

This activity tracks the plans for the data processing system capacity and performance. It provides estimating factors. It catalogs current and planned capacity use. It confirms projections and monitors implementation to assure that the needed results are achieved on a timely basis. It tracks projected capacity changes to assure that the responsible groups order and install needed capacity changes. It obtains from vendors the capacity and performance factors for new equipment in order to make the data available for estimating purposes. It prepares contingency and configuration alternatives. Success is measured by the adequacy of capacity and performance when needed. It supervises and assures the capacity and performance projections of the organization as a part of the review of the phased evolutionary process.

Data Management and Storage Planning

Data management and storage planning staff coordinates the storage architecture, design, and supporting software. Data storage security rules and techniques are specified and supervised in development and operational use. This staff catalogs the current and projected use of storage capacity; evaluates new products for inclusion in or modification of the data storage architecture and plans; is an active participant in the phased evolutionary process review; and measures storage planning success by the adequacy of storage capacity, the storage performance capabilities, and the acceptance of the architectural rules by the application and system developers.

Distributed Data Processing Architecture

Data processing units' system economics and capacity vary over a broad spectrum of capabilities and prices. Small systems have become quite powerful. Thus, there is more demand for personal data processing systems. These "distributed" or "standalone" systems are wanted on a geographically and organizationally decentralized basis. This activity sets the rules for when and how to distribute data processing. It understands the options available; catalogs the current and planned use; disseminates the rules for documentation and data base growth and use; provides operational security rules and rules for separate or interconnected operation; and reviews and confirms new project proposals and projections.

The objective of this activity is to support the growth of user-based, distributed data processing. The activity offers skilled assistance that avoids the traps for the uninitiated. Success is achieved by direct participation of this activity's staff in the phase review process, and by the growth of user-controlled data processing capacity. Properly anticipating the distributed data processing needs of the organization to achieve marketplace events is another must for this acivity's staff.

OPERATION AND CONTROL ACTIVITIES

Computer Network Management Staff

This staff operates and controls the communications network. It handles all activities, from getting vendor equipment and lines to operating the facility successfully. It is responsible for knowing at all times the status of facilities, diagnosing and isolating faults, initiating corrective action, arranging maintenance, placing alternate capabilities into action, and otherwise assuring full and appropriate network operation.

This staff orders lines and facilities. It operates services and tools to supervise the network status. It plans and schedules all network upgrading in order to achieve a timely provision of communications capacity and line types. These communications capabilities are needed to produce the new marketplace events. This staff audits and controls all applicable tariffs and service billings for accuracy and economy. It acts as a catalyst for network change to achieve better and more economical service.

Success is measured by proper operation, adequate capacity, and minimized expense. This group participates in the phase review and system development. Its most important role is to ensure that the latest computer network management tools and capabilities are put into the daily operation of the data processing system, and that these tools are included in the plans and project implementation for new events.

Security Management Staff

This group focuses on the security of the data processing system. It works closely with the audit and control activities of the financial management organization. It performs risk and exposure analysis. The group recommends lines of defense. This staff ensures that the appropriate tools and techniques are utilized. It ensures that available security equipment and architecture concepts are ordered and used. It establishes that users install a set of sensitivity tests in order to understand user security status.

The security group monitors security plans and implementation status with periodic reviews and reports to management. The group is an active participant in the phase review. Success is measured by the sensitivity of all application and system development leaders to this subject. Do development leaders include adequate security in all plans? Do the users' sensitivity tests demonstrate awareness of potential security threats and a response to expected marketplace challenges?

Installation Management

This activity catalogs, controls, and achieves the workload for the data processing system physical installation. It participates in the phase review. It works with vendors, architects, and skilled contractors; obtains early access to equipment to prepare installation plans; and refines and tests the plans for physical installation. The group relates the installation process to the available time and budget constraints. Success is measured by the correct results at the right time within the expense projections. If necessary, this group negotiates with vendors for features that can provide improved installations.

Availability Management

Availability is the ability to obtain successful operation of a work station when desired by a user. Good availability is the result of considering many factors, such as the design features of the work station, the system support program capabilities, the speed of corrective maintenance, and the education of the work station operator to good practices and work station housekeeping—to name just a few factors.

This group provides a coordinated effort to prepare a plan of action to ensure availability. It includes monitoring system elements for early warnings of difficulty. It alerts and directs appropriate staffs to proper and timely actions. The group maintains a base of statistics and experience to understand, compare, and report actual results. It requires the education of the involved development personnel to availability needs and to the corrective action options that are available. This group participates in the phase review in order to anticipate and respond to new availability needs. It negotiates with vendors to obtain equipment features and built-in hardware or software that can improve levels of availability. It requires development objectives to build availability capability into new projects. Success is indicated by the actual results, as well as by the acceptance of these responsibilities by the involved participants.

Facilities Planning

Buildings, space, operating areas, traffic areas, physical delivery, and facility issues are coordinated in this activity. This staff participates in the phase review in order to catalog future requirements and respond to them. It supervises the facilities action plans from the preproposal identification of a need to the successful operation of facilities. It coordinates the management and budgetary approval process. This activity deals with a long lead time process in the worst of cases. Therefore, an early start is absolutely necessary. Success is measured by timely achievement of the required facilities within budget plans.

DEVELOPMENT MANAGEMENT RESPONSIBILITIES

New Application Development/ Programmer Productivity

This staff projects and manages the total application development workload required and the resources that are available. This staff is an active participant in the phase review. The group contributes to the management process by helping to optimize workload and producing timely results. It seeks opportunities to use more productive approaches; for example, it seeks available application packages to combine or reduce future needs, to assign priorities better, and to allocate resources. It statistically estimates, measures, and directs the productivity improvement of application development. This staff introduces new tools and techniques to achieve the application production plan and output goals. Where possible this staff encourages the use of development alternatives, such as options that reduce the use of development resources or offer a more economic alternative. Included are efforts shared with other organizations and use of vendor or externally provided development efforts. It runs the development activities on a businesslike basis with clear project goals, measurements, and performance assessment. It is responsible for the quality of the end results and for the estimating factors used in the organization. It contributes the viability of this responsibility to the phase review.

New Users Application Development Support

There are new data processing system user requirements that are best provided by the users themselves. These are one-time jobs or small, low-use jobs that do not justify the use of professional development staffs. A broad spectrum of tools and techniques offer fast and productive application development. These methods are directly usable by members of the user departments. One method of operation is to establish an information system center that provides services with access to the latest application development tools and techniques. This center also provides skilled assistance to let users prepare their own application development services and results.

A key responsibility is to distinguish between jobs that are done best by the user and significant jobs that are done best in a professional application development department. The latter kind of job includes those that are high-volume or complex processing with highly repetitious, high-performance data base requirements. The information system center helps with important questions such as how to document security ground rules and implementation guidance. This center staff also helps the phase review. Its success is measured by the ability of users to achieve timely and economic end results on their own.

Current Program Support Group

This group assumes responsibility from the assigned development group for developed application programs. It takes over the programs when the development and implementation phases are completed. At that point this group assumes responsibility for continued successful operation and maintenance of a program. This forced change to a new responsibility group imposes a businesslike control on further changes and modifications. The objective is to free development resources while maintaining sufficient competency to achieve continued successful operation. Updating of application programs is always required. Should the original developers or a new group do the job? Which is the best economic and response time alternative to fast change in the marketplace? That decision needs to be made by a group different from the original developers. The success of this activity is measured by its ability to satisfy users with results while freeing resources for other needs. Be careful: Premature release of skilled people may start an erosion process that has a delayed impact. Once started, this transfer may not be reversible. Poor judgment in this decision process will be evident in a growing bad response from the marketplace.

Batch/Paper Processing Support Staff

The activities discussed up to this point have focused on the change to on-line system based applications. In all organizations there is an ongoing requirement to continue the current batch-type data processing activities. In fact, in some organizations the current activities may continue to grow substantially. They will grow until the new approaches are implemented, are accepted in the marketplace, and achieve their impact potential. This staff is intended to monitor such current activities, to seek further improvements in their operation, and to prepare for further changes in an orderly manner—whether the changes are for more or less "old" processing. This staff participates in the phase review. Success is measured by the ability to keep the current activities under orderly control and improving while arranging for the cost-effective demise of the current batch-type activities.

SUMMARY

This completes a review of the major implementation staffs and activities which was designed to take the nontechnical participant in the plan process through the implementation groups of the data processing system. These groups' activities need to be identified and provided to make the data processing future events occur. You need to be able to describe these activities and how they support your objectives. If you do so, you have a better opportunity to provide an organizational structure and plans that are implementable and productive. A better appreciation of the support needs leads to an understanding of the implementation trade-offs that are available. These trade-offs will be made as you test options and weigh budget constraints. Also, knowing the support needs helps you to define the numeric factors needed to make progress toward the desired marketplace events. The most important step to be taken is implementation of the phase review as an orderly and managed effort toward change. It is one thing to understand the identity and purpose of these activities; it is another to be able to successfully use, direct, and integrate these activities. These activities are needed to move the data processing system toward a productive but changing future.

CHAPTER SEVEN

Step 5: Assessing the Results

CHAPTER GOALS

Evaluate the results of the planning process.

Exercise the trade-offs needed to fine-tune the results.

Prepare for the next planning cycle.

GENERAL CONSIDERATIONS

Purpose of Assessment

Long-range planning is an iterative process. It is intended for initial quick completion followed by a planned update or planning cycle repetition within 18 to 24 months. The later planning cycles are marked by a validation of trends. Also, later planning cycles focus on a refinement of the selected marketplace events and the introduction of new data processing activities as required. Intermediate studies (between planning cycles) to augment the plan should be encouraged; they provide interim observations, actions, and results that are integrated into the next revision of the plan.

A long-range plan is a living event. It changes, grows, adjusts, and adapts itself to the realities of the marketplace. It is not an old masterpiece to be admired unchanged for a decade.

In planning process step 5, we revisit the previous major plan steps. However, this time we have the experience of having progressed through the entire process at least once. Our goal is to apply 20/20 hindsight. Knowing the intended plan results allows a reassessment of each step—of the methodology and the content. We should pose questions: Did the steps achieve their intended end results? Do the results of the individual steps fit together? Does the end result integrate into a reasonable plan of action? Does the end result achieve the numerically quantified objectives?

Productivity

Most plans and planning techniques result in forecasts of growth and change. They attempt to be self-fulfilling prophesies. The customer accounts, the transactions, the delivered services, and the product output all seem to grow. Hence, the desired marketplace events are selected to encourage and assist the growth process. In the real world, growth is not always possible; however, in the absence of a long-range planning process, the initial approach in most plans is to continue to use projections of staff and facilities requirements that worked in the past.

This will not do! Economic pressures are not forecast to disappear.

If the economy is fortunate enough to constrain inflation to 7 percent per annum, then the end result will be a doubling of inflation-related labor and facilities costs over the next decade. As in the example, there may also be a projected growth in customer accounts and transactions. If these also double in volume over the decade, you are faced with an overall growth factor of four in the cost of doing business. Hence, a growth plan by itself is not realistic. Rather, a plan is needed that focuses on productivity—even at the risk of zero staff and reduced customer growth.

The Real Opportunity

The real opportunity in the long-range planning process is to convert a substantial part of the business growth into economic return. This is achieved by introducing a sufficient amount of productivity tools, techniques, and improvements to offset the growth expected in expenses. There are many options available. Some options incorporate the latest data processing enhancements for replacing paper-intensive and labor-intensive operations. Other options allow opening new marketplace opportunities that result from using the new functions and facilities found in on-line, interactive data processing systems. Some of the new opportunities include the use of self-service capabilities, new forms of automated operation, and electronic devices to replace paper movement and handling. Our assessment process examines those "new function" results from the planning process.

Force Numerically Measured Goals

Throughout the planning process attention has been directed at quantifying marketplace events. Most events have an effect on the activities of a business. Most industries have established and accepted numeric measures of performance, and these measures may also be used to assess output. Numeric measures are needed in setting goals and measuring progress. Sometimes you may have to force the issue of numeric measuring. Generally planners avoid coming to grips with these numeric measures unless the reviewing management insists. In the example (chapter 2), these factors, their role, and purpose were shown. Your key job in the assessing management is to insist that these measures occupy a central role in describing goals and assessing progress. Your insistence on their inclusion is the only way to assure the full benefits of the planning process. Keep the measurements simple but applicable: simple ratios that reflect important bottom line results; transactions per employee that express expense changes; accounts per branch office that indicate profit potential for that operation. In other words, output per employee and accounts per business entity are simple measures that provide good insights into key business trends. Define your own, but make sure the planning process provides for those numeric values that satisfy the measurement needs.

Set Challenging Goals

A related challenge is setting tough but realistic goals for the plan. As we just observed, with any amount of customer and transaction growth you might experience a doubling of the key numeric expense factors over the next decade. The real test is the level of staff and facilities growth that you allow in order to handle that growth. Therefore, set a goal of achieving that result with essentially no net growth in the number of branches or the size of the staff, as a starting point. Only in that manner can you force a close consideration of a wide range of improvement options and alternatives.

Require Consideration
of New Data Processing Techniques

Your role as the reviewing manager is to communicate the key goals and how you plan to measure success in their attainment. This is needed to motivate and direct the participants in the planning process to recognize their challenge. The participants need to consider an array of data processing system responses to find possible improvements. The response sought should provide alternatives to the paper-intensive, manual labor operations now in use. For alternatives consider the introduction of on-line, interactive, data processing facilities and better use of the data base and data communications. Another option is the introduction of customer self-service as a good starting target for high-productivity results. Also, the ability to offer better and faster decisions with data base use and application-based processing must be considered as a productivity tool in the marketplace. Using improved work stations in less capital-intensive business structures or branches is a practical alternative. All of these improvements, and more, are worth consideration. However, they must be preceded by numerically quantified goals and success measures to provide high motivation.

How to Track Project Progress

The consideration of new tools, new techniques, and improvements should include the introduction of management phase reviews and the measurement of progress. The new project phase review lends itself to a continuous progress tracking effort. This was described in step 4, Reviewing Implementation Support (chapter 6). Phase proposals and phase completions will describe and test the progress in individual project efforts.

Tracking Changes Between Plan Cycles

You have to track progress closely for the first few planning cycles. Goals for these measurements between planning cycles include the following:

○ Validate the growth trends.

○ Test the estimates of marketplace event results.

○ Compare results and forecasts.

○ Focus on areas that are not performing up to forecast.

○ Measure marketplace competitive performance and progress.

○ Seek out and use industry guidelines for change.

Apply the Plan Every Day

An important objective of the planning process is to use its concepts and contents in daily decisions. Documenting new projects and development efforts should have the same formats and numeric characteristics as used in the growth plan process. Establish numeric measurements for use in specifying goals of departments and functional areas and activities. These numeric measures are the same as those used in the planning process and documentation. Set marketing and branch goals on a basis that allows their comparison to the plan objectives. Set up a productivity improvement "budget" for allocation and measurement of achievement. In effect, let the planning process and its documentation serve as a management tool. Use it in the day-to-day planning and measurement of individual responsibilities.

Assessing Step 1: Setting Objectives

An important recommendation in step 1 was the need for top management to make an early review and approval effort to reduce the rate of change in the subsequent planning process. However, now the time has come to reassess further the targets chosen for the planning process.

○ Did the end result support the objectives selected?

○ Are the planning process conclusions and recommendations consistent with the goals?

○ Was the result of the plan action consistent with the objective?

○ Were the opportunities significant?

○ Was the economic assessment of the projected results versus expenses good enough to proceed?

○ Were the marketplace events and timetable a reasonable response to the business area selected?

○ Do the projected plan results match the management expectations for the business area selected and for the organizational goals?

Here is the point to exercise your 20/20 hindsight. Revisiting the start of the planning process is appropriate if the end result needs fine-tuning in direction and scope. One criterion to apply is the reactions of the plan process participants in the later steps.

- ○ Did they feel comfortable with the areas and time frames selected?

- ○ Do they support the time frame for events projected in the plan?

- ○ Do they feel confident in the events and results forecast?

Beauty is in the eye of the beholder. In this case it is in the eyes of the planning process participants and their key reviewing management. Your objective is *not* necessarily to seek a consensus of all the participants in the organization. Rather, it is trying to seek agreement between the key sponsoring and reviewing managers with the sense of direction chosen and the plan content.

Assessing Step 2:
Projecting Marketplace Events

Throughout step 2, a number of tests were proposed for preparing the plan content and recommendations. We will not repeat those tests and exercise here. Rather, we examine a few key components and assess their results. The main need is to weigh the proposed marketplace actions. These future events are the key contribution from the plan process, and all results follow from that starting point. Some of the important questions to answer are:

- ○ Can the marketplace events be pretested and qualified?

- ○ Will customers respond to and support the moves?

- ○ Are the projected marketplace volumes attainable and realistic?

- ○ Can our staffs achieve the working results expected?

- Are the investment and expenses levels appropriate, and do they offer adequate return?

- Does your vendor have sufficient ability to support and deliver the necessary system resources?

- Do the time event maps represent an industry-accepted sense of direction?

If self-service is a key component, consider the following additional questions:

- Will there be an adequate number of customers willing to use self-service?

- Is the projected effort in the right geographic area?

- Will customers ask for a magnetic-striped plastic card and a personal identification number (a PIN)?

- Will the transaction volumes be justified and support the investment?

- Can you provide the right marketing support?

Concerning the work stations,

- Is the work station plan (type, quantity, and growth) realistic?

- Are the work station economics and installability feasible?

- Is the projected work station usage adequate to support the investment?

Marketplace events and actions are your prime interface to customers. These actions are your response to marketplace competition. You have dealt with and responded to competition in the past. You need to judge whether the marketplace events projected will produce the numeric measures and acceptance results projected. Do you have the commitment of the user groups, the marketing management, and the data processing management to achieve the projected end results?

Assessing Step 3:
Anticipating System Resources

The techniques used in step 3 are well established in data processing activities. The step was described to show the dependency of the system resource results on the projected marketplace events. The challenge in the future will be to ensure that the system resource projections keep up with the products of the data processing industry. The data processing industry products are evolving rapidly, with more functions and in faster and cheaper packages. These packages provide more return on your equipment purchase funds. But your solutions require an increasing sophistication and growing volume of results. Hence, it is essential that the results of this step, the growth in system resources, be reviewed with your vendor at an early point. This is necessary in order to compare the projected system resource needs with the latest trends in data processing equipment.

The early phases of the plan require detailed plans and proposals to achieve the market events and action timetables. Another important assessment is the system resource changes between successive plan cycles. Why have they changed? In what way have they changed? The new and changing requirements need to be identified, communicated, and confirmed with the implementation functions.

Assessing Step 4:
Reviewing Implementation Support

Step 4 is designed to expose you, the nontechnical participant in the planning process, to the range of support needed to implement systems successfully. To assess the results of this step consider the following:

○ Did you understand the various activities?

○ Did you understand the plans of action?

○ Did you understand the contribution of each activity to a successful implementation?

The critical common element is the proposed new project phase review. This review was basic to coordinating all the groups and their activities necessary to achieve a successful system implementation. Your role and assessment objective is thus to ascertain when and how the phase review will be provided. A continuous phase review must have support and participation of top management. This participation assures a reasonable chance of achieving the help and cooperation needed for effective evolution.

○ Will your management support such a phase review?

○ If not, is there another approach they will support?

○ If there is not a viable approach, how will you manage this multigroup, multiphase review?

○ Will the phase review work or are you going to get into deeper trouble?

○ Your assessment here is less concerned with content and more with the ability to manage in your environment.

AN OVERALL ASSESSMENT

There is an old saying: "Nothing is impossible for the other person to accomplish." A plan of large scope has potential traps.

○ Has it reached out too far or too broadly?

○ Is the plan on too fast a timetable?

○ Are there adequate skills in the organization, both managerial and technical, to implement the plan?

○ Is the plan too disruptive of current efforts?

○ Are the results too speculative?

○ Is there too little testing to assure that the projections are reasonable?

As the responsible assessing manager, your judgment must weigh the plan content and the plan team support.

My suggestion is to let the decision evolve.

- ○ Start into the implementation of the plan with the use of a project phase review.
- ○ Start building a base of knowledge and credibility.
- ○ Start measuring the phase status and phase results.
- ○ Get the facts necessary to start making orderly decisions.
- ○ If necessary, modify and amend the plan based on actual test, development, and detailed study results.

You will quickly learn whether the plan is solid and, at the time, you will be putting refined specifics into the plan and the phase review. After a point, the plan assessment starts to take care of itself. If the plan was right, the plan content will start to happen. If not, a self-correcting process will start to shift the plan content to one that will be correct. Then the plan process will start to work for your organization.

Financial Adequacy

- ○ What are the corporate goals for the financial growth of the business?
- ○ What are the capital investment plans?
- ○ What returns are expected?
- ○ Does the plan content help to achieve those objectives?

The plan process did not include a detailed economic assessment, for reasons outlined before (see page 58). However, a quick assessment test was shown in the example (chapter 2) (see page 30). These values are needed to determine the effect on capital investment funds.

- ○ If the plan shifts the time and amount of investment, is it still realistic?
- ○ Will the results support such a shift?

In any event, an overall financial assessment is required on a continuing basis. If the results of the analysis suggest change, then a plan recycle may be required. Another option is to select the plan portion that is the major user of funds. That plan segment needs to be reassessed for plan content and timing.

Unanticipated Event Capacity

Dealing with an unanticipated event requires two decisions: first, a quick assessment of the event and its potential impact; second, formulation of a responsive plan of action. The documented long-range plan provides a basis for both of these decisions. An existing plan provides a basis for evaluating external and unanticipated events. The plan provides a statement of possible actions and their timetable. The numeric measures allow a comparison with the projected results of the unanticipated event.

Another aspect is the need to determine whether there is sufficient capacity or capability to respond on a timely basis. As the planning process progressed through step 3 to a forecast of system resources, an allowance was made for contingency capacity. This was required as a safeguard against estimating inaccuracies and untested parameters. This contingency factor buys some time to respond to changes and unanticipated events—and results.

You may, in addition, turn to outside services or support groups to fill a temporary gap. That is, providing that you have a basis for relating the added procurement expense to your overall plan and resources. In general, a good planning process includes a cushion. However, early recognition of and response to an unanticipated event is a must.

WATCH OUT!

Facts of Life

In most organizations the users and the data processing departments do not communicate effectively. Each tends to do their own plans independently of the need to interrelate the long-range plans. In fact, most plans and marketplace event projections tend to be short-range, generally in a one- to two-year time frame. In most cases the numerically quantified plan goals are not set or related to specific marketplace activities. Therefore, numerically quantified result projections are needed. These allow the future event results to be compared with the objectives and goals for the organization. This comparison assures that the planning process is providing sufficient capacity or capability to respond to marketplace needs on a timely basis. This part of the process must come to grips with the numerically quantified goals if meaningful results are to be expected from the long-range data processing plan.

Potential Pitfalls

The results of several first planning cycles have been surprisingly consistent in making a significant mistake! The marketplace events have been projected with a little prompting. They have shown growth in customers, accounts, and transactions. Then the branch and staff projections have been made in order to provide the customer interface capacity to achieve those events. The planners have used past ratios that require staffs and facilities that are proportional to the growth in accounts and transactions. Hence, the first projected growth in staff is too big and is impossible to support financially because of the compound growth of transactions per staff and expense per staff. In each case, the initial response of the planners has been to take the staff growth trend of the last few years and project its continuation.

The result is an economic disaster that forces a hard confrontation between several required improvement options. Then the light comes on: Business and staff growth as usual will not work. A successful future will be achieved only through the introduction of improvements that produce much higher output per staff. The new marketplace events will have to take advantage of the emerging high-output tools and techniques, such as new types of automatic branches and extended self-service banking. When these new techniques are applied, the results become much more acceptable. A plan is perceived that provides the marketplace growth objectives with little or no growth in the conventional resources of labor and paper-intensive activities. A plan is then formulated that taps the capabilities of the new approaches, and the future starts looking brighter. All that is left to do is make it all happen within the plan and the budget constraints.

Other Surprises

Other unexpected results included the following:

CARDS

The growth in the number of plastic cards is allowed to fall behind the self-service usage projections. The user population is not at the level required to support the card-based, self-service work station and action plans.

DEVELOPMENT ACTIVITY

The application and system development resources lack measurements of output or productivity. There is a need for goals and for a plan to improve the productivity of these groups. These are needed to upgrade significantly the output from these resources if development goals are to be achieved with realistically available resources.

SYSTEM CAPACITY

System and network capacity is not being ordered according to a plan. Rather, order decisions are tied to specific events only. That is like buying a quart container of milk only after you know how each glass of milk will be used. Generally cartons of milk are bought at the going rate of consumption for the commodity. This is procurement for continuing capacity growth on an orderly basis; it allows users to have the needed capacity when required by events; it helps to eliminate last-minute decisions and procurement delays; and it helps to shorten the implementation lead times and speeds marketplace response.

PROGRESS MAY BE SLOW AT FIRST

The impact of the new electronic transactions on the growth of previous paper-intensive solutions tend to take more time than anticipated. The inherent growth in the previous paper-based solutions, although it is in the process of slowing down, can still be a considerable burden. Numeric measurements and goals need to be projected for the phasing out of the old solutions. Better estimates are needed for the transition from the old to the new.

Implementation Issues

There are generally no serious problems in getting a plan and a project phase review under way. This is true after there is an understanding of the action plan, assignments, and timetable by all the involved managers. The issues discussed here are action plan stages that need special emphasis. The typical problems, which are corrected rapidly when recognized, are as follows.

INVENTORY OF EFFORTS

The application and system development organizations may have only an incomplete inventory of the efforts under way—their status and future commitments. Activities to coordinate results with other groups tend to be absent or to come late in the process. For example, coordination between data processing and marketing, in preparation for a marketplace event, tends to occur late in the process, at best. Non–data processing management reviews of development status occur only at the end of an effort. But they should occur throughout the continuing phase review process.

NEEDS AND PRIORITIES

Both system and development resource needs are not generally projected. They are not shown as related to future projects. Priorities are poorly set, if at all. Data processing priorities are unrelated to marketplace events.

PROJECT CONTROL

The process for controlling development projects through their life cycle are, at best, not comprehensive. The process is unrelated to implementation and marketplace support functions. The phase review from product concept through postimplementation review needs to be structured. There must be understanding of the progress through each phase and a realistic criterion for "graduation" from each phase. Progress tracking is essential.

QUANTITIES

Time, effort, and funds are sometimes spent in an environment that lacks numeric measurements and goals. The environment lacks a priority setting and control process for review by management not from data processing. The implementation support review (chapter 7) is intended to be done on a nontechnical basis. This is to help the non–data processing management to understand and to control these vital functions.

A complete recommended action plan and timetable for implementation of the growth plan process appear in appendix 3.

Good News

There is good news from the planning process situations to which this process has been applied, as follows.

FAST RESULTS

Preliminary results are produced rapidly. Generally results are produced in a matter of weeks or a few months, depending on the priorities set and the scope assigned for the first efforts. The process allows and encourages a high degree of cooperation between the users and the data processing staff once everyone knows that this process will be a joint user and data processing department planning effort.

THE CHANGE

The end result of the planning process is best observed in an attitude change. The organizational debates change from "What should we do?" to "How do we get it done?" This is a much more productive environment, with much less friction and contention.

VENDORS

The role of vendors becomes better understood. The plan's content communicates your action plan and needs. The vendor helps you to achieve better support and a more timely result when he is given more lead time in understanding and responding to your needs.

THE FUTURE BECOMES MORE AUTOMATIC

In most organizations the process of achieving the future is a series of traumatic events. Many are repeated each year in the frantic chase for an annual plan. The concept of plan recycling with its self-correcting nature is the vital contribution of this planning process. When the planning process is augmented with the project phase review, it introduces a coordinated and continuing view of the future. This routinized process gains acceptance and participation by the key management. Their frustrations in being unable to articulate their future direction in an interactive manner are reduced. The cooperative interaction acts as a catalyst. It speeds the process, as well as improving the end result.

THE BEST NEWS

The long-range planning process really works!

Using the Plan

Here are some general tips to aid you in making better use of the planning output document when it becomes available.

○ It is a valuable and revealing document. Its distribution needs careful control. You may wish to restrict distribution or to limit distribution of selected parts to persons with well-identified management responsibilities.

○ Use the document to communicate direction decisions to the key management in the non–data processing departments and activities.

○ Use the plan content to stimulate complementary and supporting efforts in other activities such as marketing or manufacturing.

○ Establish areas, issues, or problems requiring interim studies and results between plan recycles.

○ Establish a calendar of key events as a device for coordination and progress measurement. Tie the key events to the marketplace events timetable.

○ Set the next plan iteration target and assign organizational responsibility early. It is best to present the timetable for the next planning cycle as part of the planning process results. It clears the air quickly on whose job it is to collect comments, suggestions, and generally get ready for the next recycle.

○ All planning process teams must be small and consist of high-level management persons. The view of the corporation from this vantage point is valuable. You may wish to use participation in the planning process as a requirement for further individual promotion and responsibilities.

CONCLUDING THOUGHTS

An old Chinese proverb says, Knowing that you have a problem is half the solution. I believe perceptive managers would agree with the proposition that the earlier they understand what is needed, the more time they have to prepare for a timely and effective solution. This guide has been intended to take the skills you have developed in a nontechnical environment and to show you how to apply them to the fast emerging world of on-line, interactive data processing. May all your future plans and solutions be timely and effective.

An Executive Presentation

Purpose: This presentation is intended for the manager responsible for the planning process to use with executives who have requested a description of the long-range planning process. The process is described in detail in this book.

THE GROWTH PLAN PROCESS: PLANNING FOR FUTURE MARKET EVENTS WITH DATA PROCESSING SUPPORT IN FINANCIAL INSTITUTIONS

Outline of Presentation

Pressures for change
Future options and examples
Formulating a plan
Why on-line financial systems?
Why plan?
How to plan?
Step 1: Setting objectives
Step 2: Projecting marketplace events
Step 3: Anticipating system and development needs
Step 4: Reviewing implementation support
Step 5: Assessing the results
Watch out for pitfalls!
With whom to plan?
Suggested action plan

Pressures for change

- Competition—inside and outside the industry
- Inflation—growing expenses and falling margins
- Customer sophistication and new or innovative products
- Technology and communications
- Deregulation—facts and acts

Future options and examples

Market or customer focus

- Retail: affluent or broad market
- Wholesale: international, national, or middle market
- Specialized customers

Geographic emphasis

- Nationwide, regional, or contiguous market
- Local, sharing, or network/interchange

Offering or product oriented

- Retail: card, self-service, or remote banking
- Wholesale: cash management, loans, or leasing
- Combinations: As in retailing—Focus on customer, needs, and location

Formulating a plan

    ○ Goal: Achieving objectives by organized use of strengths

    ○ How: Continuous process
             Systematic methodology
             Best estimates of the future
             Current decisions
             Measured progress and results
             Scheduled recycle

Before the plan process

    ○ Define the business and its goals.

    ○ Define customer and institutional needs.

    ○ Establish and select plan alternatives.

Plan content

    ○ Step 1: Select market areas, time table, and objectives.

    ○ Step 2: Project future marketplace events.

    ○ Step 3: Anticipate the system resources.

    ○ Step 4: Review the implementation support.

    ○ Step 5: Assess the results.

After the plan process

    ○ Implement the plan.

    ○ Use organization, economic, and resource strengths.

    ○ Support with marketing, technical, and systems know-how.

Why on-line financial systems?

More productivity options

- ○ Direct teller support
- ○ Self-service
- ○ New branching alternatives

New and extended service options

- ○ Remote banking
- ○ Communications and network based services
- ○ Shared and distributed services

Change to future banking

- ○ Alternatives to paper
- ○ Direct posting of accounts
- ○ Removal of regulatory and geographic constraints
- ○ Improved security
- ○ Open new cost/price/benefit structures

Why plan?

Marketplace actions constrained by

○ Need for setting events

○ Available development resources

○ Time from decision to implementation

Effective data processing evolution requires

○ Recognition of key decisions

○ Examination of alternatives

○ Setting goals and priorities

○ Maximize development resource use

○ Ordering future system capacity to plan

○ Measuring progress and resource use

Effective bank management requires

○ Communication of direction

○ Relating user to data processing

○ Earlier and better decisions

○ Basis for assessing external events

○ Tracking plan results

How to plan?

Step 1: Setting objectives

Areas: Start with a reasonable goal (such as one area)

- Select retail, corporate, trust, international, or correspondents, etc.
- For the selected area: pick segments and targets, such as retail: branch structure, self-service, remote banking, etc.
- Introduce and assign the plan process team.

Time frame: minimum of 6 years (facility lead time)

- Try four 1-year periods followed by three 2-year periods.
- Too far out?
  Assume current trends will continue.
  Plan the new events and add to the current trends.
  Reexamine in 1 to 2 years.

Objectives—first plan

- Involve the key parties.
- Develop the plan structure and tools.
- Assign the management responsibilities.
- Develop an evolution base for the selected area.
- Danger! You must complete and stop refining.

Objectives—second plan

- For the selected area:
  Validate trends.
  Refine content.
  Focus on key areas.
- Initiate plans for additional area actions.

Step 2: Projecting marketplace events

Customers/accounts/transactions (by time frame)

○ Type, growth, volume

○ Plastic: type, growth, volumes

Branch structure/staff/function

○ Size, staff/function, accounts, and transactions

○ Geographic/demographic coverage: customer type and volumes, radius of coverage

Application/marketing program definition

○ Start with selected areas and segments (step 1), such as retail: branch, self-service (see table A1–1), remote banking.

○ Establish event timing and sequence for each area.

○ Pilot stages are not required for all efforts.

○ Complete similar tables for each selected area.

○ Re-sort all events by year.

Table A1–1

KEY EVENTS	EVENT YEAR FOR SELF–SERVICE						
	1	2	3	4	5/6	7/8	9/10
ATMs	Pilot	Start	→	End	—	—	—
Lobby inquiry	—	Start	End	—	—	—	—
Automatic branch	—	—	—	—	Start	→	End
Telephone banking	—	—	—	Pilot	Start	End	—
Statement banking	—	—	—	—	—	Start	End

Establish work stations

- ○ Functional description
- ○ Users and locations
- ○ Installation rates

Numerically measure future events

- ○ Work stations
- ○ Users/plastic
- ○ Transaction volumes, such as active cards × transaction volumes

Measure output or productivity trends

- ○ Transactions/employee
- ○ Accounts/branch
- ○ Funds/employee
- ○ Activity/work station

Step 3: Anticipating system and development needs

- ○ Work stations → Terminals
- ○ Transactions → Messages
- ○ Messages → Network load
- ○ Messages → Processor load
  Including development, testing, and backup
- ○ Accounts/customers → Storage requirements
  Including work areas, file generations, and backup
- ○ Application → Development needs
  New and existing projects
  Programming productivity estimates
- ○ Quantities that need testing and refinement:
  Rate of growth
  Application load/system growth
  Backup capacity reconfiguration

Step 4: Reviewing implementation support

For each area

- Who has the responsibility?
- Current objectives and timetable
- Assigned budgets and staff vs. goals
- When and how reviewed by management

Management and planning

- Combined user/DP planning process
- New project phase review management process

System design and evolution

- System architecture
- Network architecture
- Capacity and performance assurance
- Data storage and management
- Distributed data processing

Operations and control

- Computer network management
- Security management
- Installation management
- Availability management
- Facilities plans

Development function management

- New application development
- New users support
- Programming productivity
- Batch/paper process evolution

Step 5: Assessing the results

Productivity results: Account/transaction growth
vs. branch/staff results

Key events and marketplace results

- ○ Timely and appropriate results vs. development and resource commitments
- ○ Ability to test and qualify key moves

System resource growth

- ○ Reasonable planning factors
- ○ Capacity confirmation and acquisition

Plan recycle

- ○ When, why, and by whom?
- ○ Is the new project management process working?
- ○ Other functional plans interact and coordinate?

Watch out for pitfalls!

Usual plans before this plan process

    ○ Short range—1 to 2 years

    ○ Do not relate market and DP events

Big surprises in input to the plan process

    ○ Branch staff vs. account/transaction growth

    ○ Plastic growth vs. self-service use

    ○ Application development load vs. resource

    ○ System capacity need vs. resource

    ○ (Paper-unimpacted vs. -impacted growth—not an on-line activity, but usually a batch activity)

Implementation support input to the plan process

    ○ Poor inventory and control of efforts

    ○ Management process missing for new projects

    ○ Priorities and resources not understood

    ○ Status at point in time not documented

With whom to plan?

- ○ Top management sponsor
- ○ Marketplace planning
- ○ Data processing planning
- ○ Industry know-how
- ○ Systems know-how
- ○ Growth plan process facilitator
- ○ Persons reporting to top management

Suggested action plan

Small but high-level task force

Users and data processing

Phased plan and timetable

- ○ Step 1: a few days (area, objectives, and goals)
- ○ Step 2: 3 to 5 weeks (future marketplace plans)
- ○ Management review

- ○ Step 3: 3 to 5 weeks (system and development needs)

- ○ Step 4: 1 to 2 weeks (system implementation)
- ○ Management review

- ○ Step 5: 1-week assessment and final report
- ○ Management review

◯

◯

A Long-Range Planning
Report Outline

Purpose: This outline is presented as a guide to the type of content that is to be documented. It also presents the results of the planning process in a logical sequence. Suggested formats and tables are included.

Summary for Managers

Introduction
  Planning team members
  Planning time frame
  Determining business areas covered
  Planning objectives
Highlights and summary of content
  Key marketplace projections
    Branches and staffs
    Staff and branch output
    Accounts and transactions
    Growth trends
    Changes from prior plans
    Key events time maps
    List of yearly event start dates
    Plastic cards and media projections:
      Growth volumes
      Changes from prior plans
    Work stations:
      Growth volumes
      Changes from prior plans
  Anticipation of system resources
    Transaction and message volume trends:
      Growth volumes
      Changes from prior plans
    System resource trends:
      Growth volumes
      Changes from prior plans
  Implementation issues
    New issues
    Prior issues and status
  Assessment
    The plan process
      Methodology
      Time, effort, and participation
    Plan and results:
      Key trends vs. goals
      Key value results

Recommendations
   Planning process follow-up and assignments
   Critical issues identified
   Priority issues and recommendations

THE REPORT CONTENT

The plan report is the plan of record. The volumes and key values shown are based on the results of the protected future events. Current event volumes and results are shown as the expected results prior to the future events taking place.

The plan report should include a set of assumptions for all key values. The assumptions should include their source and the planning team's level of confidence in the assumptions.

PROJECTING MARKETPLACE EVENTS

Branches and Staffs

Table A2-1 shows branch and staff plans based on the future events. A current events population trend table may be included for comparison.

This table is used to describe the staff by task type or job. These values will be used later to set the work station counts.

Repeat this table for each year. This will show the staff growth trends by task type.

Table A2-1

| | TOTAL STAFF SIZE | | | | | | |
| | | | BY TASK TYPE | | | | |
	Range	Average	1	2	3	4	N
Branch size							
Large							
Medium							
Small							
Automatic							
Off-premise							
Mini							
Etc.							
Total staff for each task type							

Staff and Branch Growth

For all plan years and future events, table A2–2 shows the total branch and staff population over the plan period. These are key values. They show the staff needed to achieve the required output levels. These are the output levels needed to handle customer, account, and usage growth over the plan period.

This table may be used for branch totals and department staff totals. The table may be repeated for other user groups with large staffs and changes.

Account Growth for All Plan Years

Table A2–3 is used to describe the growth of accounts by type during the plan period. The total number of customer accounts will be less than the total by account type, because customers usually have more than one account; for example, in banking a customer may have a savings account and a checking account.

This table may be repeated to show account or customer types in other business areas.

Future Event Time Maps

Table A2–4 can be applied to each business area in the plan. Each future event should show the years of the pilot test, the installation start, and the end. Not all events require pilots.

Table A2–2

	NUMBER OF BRANCHES	STAFF SIZE BY YEAR						
		-3	-2	-1	1	2	3	N
Branch size								
Large								
Medium								
Small								
Etc.								
Total staff								
% annual staff growth								
% overall staff growth								
since year -1								

Table A2–3

| | CUSTOMER ACCOUNTS BY YEAR | | | | | | |
	−3	−2	−1	1	2	3	N
Account type							
Retail							
Commercial							
Trust							
International							
Etc.							
Total customer accounts							
% annual growth in customer accounts							
% overall growth in customer accounts since year −1							

Yearly Future Event Start Date Project List

Table A2–5 is a list for all future event start dates. It is obtained by sorting all future event time map entries for all time maps into one sequence by year of occurrence.

Plastic Card Population

Table A2–6 is provided for each medium or card type; for example, plastic cards, paper checks, and passbooks are worth listing.

Plastic Card Activity

Card activity is an important factor needed to assure success for some future events. Self-service banking, for example, is an important area that needs a large and growing card base with active card use. See table A2–7.

Table A2–4

| | YEAR | | | | | |
BUSINESS AREA FUNCTION	1	2	3	4	5	N
	Key Events (Pilot, Start, End)					
Teller automation						
Self-service						
Branch automation						
Etc.						

Table A2-5

YEAR OF OCCURRENCE	BUSINESS AREA	FUTURE EVENT	START DATE
1			
2			
3			
N			

Work Stations

Total work station usage volumes for setting system resources are obtained from the individual work station populations and usage. The card based usage is used as a cross check on work station totals. The card based work stations (automatic teller machines), times their usage volumes, should be equal to or less than the active card usage volumes. If they are far apart then some action is needed to reduce the difference.

Work Station Description

For each type of work station the following data are needed:

EMPLOYEE OR STAFF
WORK STATION CHARACTERISTICS

For each type of work station list the following: input, display, output, and media (such as bank card stripe reader).

Table A2-6

	MEDIA POPULATION BY YEAR						
	-3	-2	-1	1	2	3	N
Medium type							
1							
2							
3							
N							
Total for all media							
% annual growth in media population							
% overall growth in media population since year -1							

Table A2–7

| | MEDIA USAGE STATISTICS BY YEAR | | | | | | |
	−3	−2	−1	1	2	3	N
Media activity							
Active cards							
Active PINs							
Total							
Transactions/active card/month							
Total card transactions/month							

RELATIONSHIP OF USER TO WORK STATION

The relation by type of user or skill area and by type of work station should be listed.

CUSTOMER OR SELF–SERVICE WORK STATION CHARACTERISTICS

For each type of work station, list a description of input, display, output, and media function.

Work Station Counts

The key input to table A2–8 is the relationship between the work station count and the branch and staff or skill types.

The work station count in this table is fixed as of the end of the installation effort. Later tables are based on the required installation counts. These counts are shown in table A2–9.

Table A2–8

| WORK STATION TYPE | WORK STATION COUNT PER BRANCH SIZE | | | | |
	LARGE	MEDIUM	SMALL	AUTOMATIC	ETC.
1					
2					
3					
N					

Table A2-9

	PERCENTAGE OF WORK STATIONS INSTALLED BY YEAR						
	−3	−2	−1	1	2	3	N
Work station type and usage							
1							
2							
3							
N							
% annual growth in work stations intalled							
% overall growth in work stations installed since year −1							

Work Station Installation Rate

The key value for table A2-9 is the rate at which the installations can be achieved. This table shows the phase events (pilot, start, etc.) and the total percentage of work station installation counts.

Installed Work Station Population

The installed work station count (table A2-10) is set by combining data from tables A2-2, A2-8, and A2-9. The number of

Table A2-10

	POPULATION OF WORK STATIONS INSTALLED BY YEAR						
	−3	−2	−1	1	2	3	N
Work station type							
1							
2							
3							
N							
Total for all work station types							
% annual growth in work stations installed							
% overall growth in work stations installed since year −1							

Table A2-11

	WORK STATION USAGE RATES BY YEAR						
	-3	-2	-1	1	2	3	N
	Average Monthly Usage Per Work Station Type						
Work station type							
1							
2							
3							
N							
% annual growth							
% overall growth since year -1							

branches by size times the work station count per branch size times the percentage installed gives the population installed.

Work Station Usage Rates

The usage rates in tables A2-11 and A2-12 show the buildup in work station installations. This increase in use is based on experience or actual marketplace acceptance. See the example (chapter 2) for typical buildup rates for teller automation and automatic teller machines.

Table A2-12

	WORK STATION USAGE RATES BY YEAR						
	-3	-2	-1	1	2	3	N
	Average Monthly Usage Per Application Area						
Application area							
Branch ATM							
Automated branch ATM							
Remote ATM							
Etc.							
% annual growth							
% overall growth since year -1							

Table A2-13

BUSINESS AREA	BRANCH ACTIVITY BY PLAN YEAR						
	-3	-2	-1	1	2	3	N
Total accounts							
Transactions/account							
Accounts/branch							
Funds/branch							
Transactions/branch staff							
Transaction/task type							
Funds/branch staff							

Work Station Usage Growth

The usage totals are from the installed work station count multiplied by the rates of work station usage.

Branch Output Analysis

These are a number of measures of branch output (see table A2-13). These are taken after the future events have been added to the action plan.

Branch and Staff Growth

Current event results are compared with the impact of the future events (table A2-14).

Current event numbers are obtained by using the base year

Table A2-14

BUSINESS AREA	PLAN YEAR						
	-3	-2	-1	1	2	3	N
Current events							
Branches (totals)							
Staffs (totals)							
Future events							
Branches (totals)							
Staffs (totals)							
Impact							
Branches (totals)							
Staffs (totals)							

(−1) output numbers. They are applied to the usage volumes for the entire plan period. A second table may be used to show the changes resulting from each of the future events.

Economic Assessment

The following format will present a general economic assessment:

Cost avoidance, cost reduction, or added revenue
   Improvement numeric measurement
   Improvement value

Expense of implementation
   Expense area numeric measurement
   Expense area value

Ratio of savings to expense
   Improvement value to expense value

ANTICIPATING SYSTEM RESOURCES

Message volume assumptions based on average volumes are shown in table A2–15. The transition to message conversion assumptions and peak-to-average volume ratios are shown in table A2–16.

Table A2–15

	AVERAGE MONTHLY MESSAGE VOLUMES BY YEAR						
	−3	−2	−1	1	2	3	N
Application/work station type							
1							
2							
N							
Total volume							
% annual growth							
% overall growth since year −1							

Table A2-16

APPLICATION/ WORK STATION	TRANSACTION: MESSAGE CONVERSION RATIO	PEAK: AVERAGE VOLUME RATIO
Type 1	1.0:3.0	1.5:1.0
Type 2	(3 messages/	(peak at 150%)
Type N	transaction)	

Message Volumes

Message volumes are shown in average or peak volumes, as specified, for a period of time, usually a month. Table A2-15 may be repeated for peak message volumes (message per month). In addition, provide a table of message arrivals per second. These are for use in getting the processor and network loading.

This table of message volumes may benefit from a geographic analysis of message volumes. This is message traffic between two or more center points. This gives added data for setting communications line and network message capacity needs.

Processing Requirements

Processing capacity is shown in instruction executions per second. One form frequently used is MIPS—millions of instruction executions per second. There are several ways of defining MIPS, so it is important to establish one definition and then use it.

The processing load is expressed in total MIPS for each major application area. This is computed from the average message volumes documented for each application area. Sometimes peak MIPS occur during the same periods for several areas. This combined occurrence may be large enough to consume the contingency processing capacity. If so, peak MIPS should be used for table A2-17 and the table labeled accordingly.

Projected Development Needs

The program development resource is projected in person-months of effort. This is estimated from several complexity factors: Is it a new effort? Is it highly interactive? And so forth.

Table A2-17

	TOTAL INSTRUCTION EXECUTIONS PER SECOND BY YEAR (MIPS)						
	-3	-2	-1	1	2	3	N
Application type							
1							
2							
N							
Total applications							
Other processing							
Development/Testing							
New applications							
Information center use							
Etc.							
Total active processing							
Backup/Contingency							
allowance							
Total processing							
% annual growth in processing (MIPS)							
% overall growth in processing (MIPS) since year -1							

Table A2-18

	DEVELOPMENT NEEDS (PERSON-MONTHS) BY YEAR						
	-3	-2	-1	1	2	3	N
Development area							
New project 1							
New project 2							
New project 3							
New project N							
Total new projects							
Other needs							
Maintenance							
Education							
New techniques							
Etc.							
Total of all needs							
% annual growth in staff needs							
% overall growth in staff needs since year -1							

Table A2-19

	PRODUCTIVITY (PERSON-MONTHS) BY YEAR						
	−3	−2	−1	1	2	3	N
Development area							
New projects							
Old projects							
Total output							
% annual growth							
% overall growth since year −1							

These factors are well known in the development planning area. Note the line item in table A2-18 for maintenance of existing programs. This is especially important as up to 75 percent of the total resource may be devoted to this category. If so, then it may be desirable to show the category broken into its major components.

Program Development Productivity

Generally programmer productivity is measured in programming output per unit of person effort. These measures are established in program estimating activities. The objective in table A2-19 is to present the continued improvement in the output of personnel in the development activities.

Projected Data Storage

Table A2-20 may be used for data storage capacity. A separate but similar table may be used for tape or mass storage requirements.

IMPLEMENTATION ISSUES

New Issues

- ○ Area
- ○ Issue
- ○ Alternative solutions

Table A2-20

	DATA STORAGE CAPACITY BY YEAR (100 MEGABYTES)						
	−3	−2	−1	1	2	3	N
Application type							
1							
2							
N							
Total application							
Other needs							
Development/Testing							
New applications							
Information center use							
Etc.							
Total active storage							
Backup/Contingency requirements							
Multigeneration master file storage							
Total storage required							
% annual growth in storage capacity							
% overall growth in storage capacity since year −1							

○ Considerations

○ Conclusion and priority recommendations

Existing Issues from Prior Plans

PRIORITY ISSUES

○ Issue identification

○ Summary

○ Current status

OTHER ISSUES

○ Issue identification

○ Summary

○ Current status

Growth Plan Process— Recommended Action Plan

Getting Started

Identify sponsor
Designate principal participants and their assistants
  Marketing/user
  Data processing
  Others
Designate the vendor participants
  Marketing
  Systems
  Growth plan process facilitator
Designate secretary
  The word processing to be used
  Report preparation responsibility
  Responsibility for the plan output documentation
Preliminary agreements
  Timetable for plan process duration
  Action plan content agreement

THE ACTION PLAN

STEP 1: SELECT MARKETPLACE AREAS, SET TIME FRAMES, AND SET OBJECTIVES

DURATION: one half day of week 1
METHOD

- Discussion with sponsor and/or principals

- Principals discussion and sponsor agreement

DOCUMENTATION: discussion factors, decisions, and groups to be involved

STEP 2: PROJECTING MARKETPLACE EVENTS

Note: The data processing participant must participate in all principal meetings of step 2.
DURATION: five weeks (weeks 1 to 5), principal meetings in weeks 1, 3, and 5
METHOD

○ Week 1 meeting: report content outline prepared

Customer/account status and expected growth: (1) if no change, (2) after future event impact

Marketing/customer interface numeric measurement: (1) locations before and after change impact, (2) staffs before and after change impact, (3) skills before and after change impact

Future event time maps: (1) major scenario areas, events, and timing; (2) impact factor estimates; (3) related events: cards, checks, geography

Identify work stations and users: (1) brief functional description of each work station, (2) work station/users model: who and how many?

Numerically measured impact of time maps: (1) customer/accounts, (2) marketing interface, (3) work stations

Test of results: (1) customer and account growth per staff and marketing location, (2) output and funds managed growth per staff and marketing location

Week 3 meeting preparation: (1) specify and assign customer/account status and expected growth, marketing/customer interface numeric measurement, and future event time maps for current values and trends; (2) estimate/draft current values for customer/account status and expected growth and marketing/customer interface numeric measurement; (3) draft current plan for future event time maps; (4) review list of other future event time maps; (5) set dates for week 3 meeting

○ Week 3 meeting

> Review collected results for customer/account status and expected growth and marketing/customer interface numeric measurement.
>
> Finalize selections for future event time maps.
>
> Consider brief presentations by product groups and/or vendor experts on the key future events, such as cards and checks.
>
> Finalize selections for future event time maps.
>
> Review estimates of impact and work station needs for identify work stations and users and numerically measured impact of time maps.
>
> Make assignments to finalize and document customer/account status and expected growth, marketing/customer interface numeric measurement, and future event time maps.
>
> Make assignments to make drafts identify work stations and users, numerically measured impact of time maps, and test of results.

○ Week 5 meeting

> Review drafts for identify work stations and users, numerically measured impact of time maps, and test of results.
>
> Consider brief presentations by experts if needed.
>
> Finalize selections for all drafts of step 2.
>
> Finalize test results for test of results.
>
> Set appointment to get sponsor agreement on step 2 results.
>
> Review documentation of assumptions and results of step 2.
>
> Start step 3 as conclusion to week 5 meeting.

STEP 3: SYSTEM RESOURCES AND DEVELOPMENT NEEDS

Note: The principal user must participate in all meetings of step 3.

DURATION: part of week 5 through week 9, principal meetings in weeks 5, 7, and 9

METHOD: Same as step 2. The assisting experts may expand to include planners for capacity and performance, development, and network planning.

○ Week 5 meeting to outline report content

Estimate resources: (1) work stations to terminals; (2) messages to network load; (3) messages and applications to processor load; (4) applications, accounts, and transactions to data storage.

Estimate development workload: (1) new efforts (this may require assumptions of complexity, (2) current efforts, (3) maintenance efforts, (4) outside or contract efforts and users' own efforts.

Make assignments.

Draft current status (years − 4 to − 1).

Review future events and work station estimates for changes, assumption assessments, or impact alteration.

○ Week 7 meeting

Review initial results of week 5 assignments.

Consider brief presentations by key groups or experts on plans, statuses, and/or projections.

Revise event timing or content as needed.

Make assignments to complete step 3.

○ Week 9 meeting

Review and complete all drafts, assumptions, and documentation.

Test results including a preliminary economic assessment.

Set appointment to get sponsor agreement on step 3 results.

Start step 4 in the week 9 meeting.

STEP 4: SYSTEM IMPLEMENTATION

Note: User and data processing principals must participate in all major meetings of step 4.

DURATION: part of week 9 through week 11, principal meetings in weeks 9 and 11

METHOD: same as previous steps. Assisting experts may expand to include operations, architecture, and development.

○ Week 9 meeting

Present report outline.
Make assignments.
Draft current status.

○ Week 11 meeting

Review drafts.
Consider brief presentations on status, plans, and/or estimates, as needed.
Identify issues; set priorities by consensus of principals.
Draft response and priority assignment to take issue action.
Complete all drafts, assumptions, and documentation.
Start step 5 during week 11 meeting.

STEP 5: ASSESSMENT AND FINAL REPORT PREPARATION

DURATION: part of week 11 and through week 13
METHOD: same as previous steps

○ Week 11 meeting

Review plan process goals and objectives from step 1.

Select and assign tests.

Draft step 5 results, report, and management summary.

Make assignments.

Draft presentation to sponsor.

Draft recommendations for post–planning process assignments.

Draft dates and participants for post–planning process and next planning process recycle assignments.

○ Week 13 meeting

Review and complete all documents including management summary.

Complete presentation to sponsor.

Issue final report.

Set plan for next planning cycle and post–planning process.

Index

Branch tellers (*cont.*)
  output, example of, 14
  staff growth, example of, 15
Branch usage
  activity, example of, 12–13
  indicators, 13
Branches
  automation of as example, 41
  output analysis, report on, 161
  output improvements, 40
Branches and staffs; *see also* Branch
    tellers
  report on, 154
  report on growth in, 155, 161–162
Bridge between user and data proc-
    essing, 44
Business area selection and long-
    range planning, 40, 44, 48
Buying output results, example of,
    31–32

Capacity and performance assur-
    ance, 107–108
Cards, plastic
  report on, 156
  surprises, 128
Cash management by banks, 46
Charting processing load, 85
Checkpoints in plan process, 51
Combined-option savings, 20–23, 25
Computer network management, 109
Constraints, 43–49
Conversion
  applications to data processing
    needs, 89–92
  ATM transactions to messages,
    33–35
  messages to processing load, 83–
    85
  teller transactions to messages, 33
  transactions to messages, 76–82
  work stations to messages, 32–33
Cost avoidance, example of, 30–31
Cost-intensive activity, 46
Coverage of shared areas, 67
Current activities, 68
Current program support group, 112
Customers for marketplace events,
    67–68
Current trends, 58–66
  example of, 11–12
  in key values, 59

in market areas, 58–66
period and usage, 59–60

Data management and storage plan-
    ning, 108
Data processing (DP)
  bridge to users, 44
  choosing new capabilities, 42
  effective development, 43
  everyone is data processing man-
    agement, 3
  needs for applications, 89–92
  new techniques required, 118
  role, 2
  timely implementation, 7
  users, joint plans with, 70
  using new capabilities, 42
  using resource capabilities, 42
Data storage
  capacity, 37
  documentation, 91–92
  projecting needs, 90–91
Dating of future events, 57
Design and evolution responsibili-
    ties, 106–109
  capacity and performance, 107
  data management and storage, 108
  distributed DP architecture, 108
  general role, 106
  implementation support, 102, 106
  network architecture and design,
    107
  system architecture, 106
Development
  anticipating resources for, 4, 73–
    93, 123, 144, 172
  effective, 43
  projecting needs, 85, 88–89, 172
  surprises in development activity,
    128
Development management, 111–113
  of batch/paper processing, 113
  current programs, 112–113
  implementation support, 102, 111
  new application development, 111
  new user applications, 112
  of programmer productivity, 111
Distributed DP architecture, 108
Documentation
  data storage capacity, 91–92
  formats, 103
  messages, 79